MONGOLIAN-ENGLISH
ENGLISH-MONGOLIAN
Dictionary & Phrasebook

Dictionary & Phrasebooks

Albanian
Arabic (Eastern) *Romanized*
Australian
Azerbaijani
Basque
Bosnian
Breton
British
Cajun French
Chechen
Croatian
Czech
Danish
Esperanto
Estonian
Finnish
French
Georgian
German
Greek
Hebrew *Romanized & Script*
Hungarian
Igbo
Ilocano
Irish

Italian
Japanese *Romanized*
Lao *Romanized*
Lingala
Malagasy
Maltese
Mongolian
Nepali
Norwegian
Pilipino (Tagalog)
Polish
Québécois
Romansch
Russian *Revised*
Shona
Slovak
Somali
Spanish (Latin American)
Swahili
Swedish
Tajik
Thai *Romanized*
Turkish
Ukrainian
Uzbek

MONGOLIAN-ENGLISH
ENGLISH-MONGOLIAN
Dictionary & Phrasebook

Aariimaa Baasanjav Marder

Hippocrene Books Inc.
New York

ISBN 0-7818-0958-4

For information, address:
Hippocrene Books, Inc.
171 Madison Avenue
New York, New York 10016

Cataloging-in-Publication data available from the Library of Congress.

Printed in the United States of America.

CONTENTS

PREFACE

The present book is a practical and concise language guide for English-speaking travelers to Mongolia. It allows the user to navigate with ease and confidence through what might otherwise prove to be a daunting linguistic and cultural experience. Mongolian vocabulary and phrases are given in both the Roman alphabet and the Mongolian Cyrillic script, enabling the user to pronounce words easily while becoming familiar with the script.

An introduction to the language and grammar gives clear, non-technical explanations with examples of usage, as well as providing an introduction to the Mongolian alphabet and sound system. A 2,000-word Mongolian-English and English-Mongolian dictionary offers essential vocabulary. The extensive phrasebook contains twelve topical chapters dealing with real-life situations that a traveler may encounter: at a hotel, at the marketplace, food and drink, entertainment, traveling within Mongolia, etc. Helpful hints regarding Mongolian national traditions and lifestyle complete this guide.

Writing this book has been a labor of love, joy, and national pride. Consequently, the author would be most interested in readers' feedback, in particular, constructive comments.

Good luck in Mongolia!

Aariimaa Baasanjav Marder
aariimaa@hotmail.com

INTRODUCTION TO THE MONGOLIAN LANGUAGE

Mongolian is a subgroup of the Altaic language family. Virtually all citizens of the country of Mongolia (formerly, Outer Mongolia, population 2.5 million people) speak Mongolian. Not all ethnic Mongolians in what was formerly referred to as Inner Mongolia (in north China) and in the Buryatia Republic (in Russia near Lake Baikal) speak Mongolian. In fact, Mongolians who live beyond the borders of Outer Mongolia speak some very old varieties of Mongolian which have developed into proper languages in their own right.

Ancient scripts and manuscripts have been discovered in Outer Mongolia that are over 2,000 years old.

Over the course of centuries, Mongols experimented with various writing systems, and as early as the thirteenth century, during the reign of Chinggis Khan's vast and great empire, Mongols knew how to write. Evidence of such a momentous historical achievement is attested to in a unique document—*The Secret History of the Mongols*—widely considered an outstanding book of a bygone civilization.

In the thirteenth century a Mongolian monk by the name of Phagba developed an alphabet which combined features of Tibetan and Chinese. In 1686, the Mongolian monk and scholar Bogd Zanabazar designed the Soyombo alphabet, which was in use for a considerable time. An example of this script can be seen on the emblem of the state banner of Mongolia (two columns, a Yin and Yang symbol between them and a spark becoming a flame to symbolize the freedom and safety of Mongolia).

Under the influence of Lamaist Buddhism, Mongolia used the Tibetan letters directly to spell out Mongolian words.

In the beginning of the sixteenth century the horizontal Mongolian script was replaced by the vertical Uigurjin Mongol script. Mongolians officially used this script until the 1940s.

In the 1940s, the then Mongolian People's Republic started using a modified Russian Cyrillic alphabet which was extended by two vowel symbols, ö and ü, the feminine counterparts of o and u. Mongolian Cyrillic has 35 letters: 20 consonants, 13 vowels and 2 signs ("hard" and "soft"). The orthography of Cyrillic Mongolian is based on the Khalkh dialect. Despite a few orthographic inadequacies, the Cyrillic system is the major vehicle of written communication today in Mongolia; virtually all newspapers, books, etc. are printed in Cyrillic letters. There has been an effort to improve literacy over many years and the result can be seen in the fact that now almost 100 percent of the population are literate.

To understand how written and spoken Mongolian have continued to develop, it is useful to take a look at the way words are formed in Mongolian. Here are examples that show two prominent characteristics of Mongolian: agglutination (the addition of affixes to words to modify their meanings or create new ones) and vowel harmony (see the pronunciation and spelling section).

өнөөдөр [ö-nÖH-dör] to<u>day</u>
өчигдөр [ö-chig-dör)] yester<u>day</u>
уржигдар [ur-jig-dar] the day before yester<u>day</u>
нөгөөдөр [nö-gÖH-dör] the <u>day</u> after tomorrow

Words and word combinations which came into being owing to characteristic features of the lifestyle of nomads and animal herders comprise a significant part of the Mongolian word stock. For example, the English concept of "domestic animal" has its Mongolian equivalent in the word мал [mal]. However, the Mongolian word is broad in its significance since it encompasses a total of five different muzzled animals, both cold-muzzled (camel and goat) and warm-muzzled (horse, sheep and cow). Stylistically, there is also a significant difference between the two languages. In English, "domestic animal" is neutral in tone, whereas Mongolian мал is an honorific.

Nomadic herders change their location seasonally. Thus, each of the four seasons is spent in a different place: autumn намаржаа [na-mar-jAH], spring хаваржаа [kha-var-jAH], winter өвөлжөө [ö-völ-jÖH] and summer зуслан [zus-lan].

In addition, tools, traditions and names of all the different types of animals, dairy products, etc. make up a considerable part of a Mongolian's vocabulary.

унага [u-na-ga] foal
даага [dAH-ga] one-year-old horse
хязаалан [khya-zAH-lan] two-year-old horse
соёолон [so-yo-lon] three-year-old horse
азарга [a-zar-ga] stallion
гүү [güh] mare
үрээ [ü-rEH] young mare
байдас [bai-das] a mare who has given birth twice

Over recent times, as a result of scientific breakthroughs, the Mongolian language has seen a great influx of borrowed words and expressions. Nevertheless, Mongolians attempt to preserve the integrity of their language by creating their own versions of borrowed words. Do not be surprised if you hear in Mongolian commonly used English words e.g., computer, radio, hard disk, compact disc, which look and sound like Mongolian words, but are actually phonetically transposed English words.

ALPHABET AND PRONUNCIATION

More than seven million people speak Mongolian—three million of them live in Inner Mongolia (in the Chinese People's Republic), 1.5 million live in the Russian Republic, and 2.5 million live in Outer Mongolia. Mongolian speakers in each nation have their own dialect and accent.

In this dictionary and phrasebook we will be discussing the Khalkh dialect, which is spoken by people living in the central part of Outer Mongolia.

Approximately ten national minorities live in Outer Mongolia, and they differ from each other in dialect, as well as in traditions and customs.

Despite inherent differences, from the point of view of someone from Outer Mongolia, the Khalkh dialect is the basis of modern Mongolian. Inasmuch as Mongolian is one of the most ancient languages in the world, it has a long and rich history, extensive vocabulary, and idioms, proverbs and sayings that reflect the life and customs of nomads.

Letter of alphabet		Approximate pronunciation	Phonetic transcription
А	а	like "a" in father	[a]
Б	б	like "b" in baby	[b]
В	в	like "v" in visa	[v]
Г	г	like "g" in great	[g]
Д	д	like "d" in dot	[d]
Е	е	like "ye" in yes	[ye]
Ё	ё	like "yaw" in yawn	[yo]
Ж	ж	like "j" in Jim	[j]
З	з	like "z" in zip	[z]

Letter of alphabet		Approximate pronunciation	Phonetic transcription
И	и	like "i" in bit	[i]
Й	й	(encountered only in diphthongs or long ii)	
К	к	like "k" in kid	[k]
Л	л	like "l" in lamb	[l]
М	м	like "m" in mom	[m]
Н	н	like "n" in nick	[n]
О	о	like "o" in dog	[o]
Ө	ө	close to "i" in bird	[ö]
П	п	like "p" in papa	[p]
Р	р	like "rr" [trilled]	[r]
С	с	like "s" in sea	[s]
Т	т	like "t" in Tom	[t]
У	у	like "oo" in pool	[u]
Ү	ү	like "u" in Susan	[ü]
Ф	ф	like "f" in far	[f]
Х	х	like "ch" in German Bach	[kh]
Ц	ц	like "ts" in tsetse fly	[ts]
Ч	ч	like "ch" in chest	[ch]
Ш	ш	like "sh" in shop	[sh]
Щ	щ	like "sh" in sheep	[sh]
Ъ	ъ	hard sign	[']
Ы	ы	like "i" in bit	[y]
Ь	ь	soft sign	[i]
Э	э	like "e" in pet	[e]
Ю	ю	like the word "you"	[yu]
Я	я	like "ya" in yarn	[ya]

Long Vowels

Vowels	Approximate pronunciation	Phonetic transcription
аа	like "a" in slow pronunciation of arm	[ah]
оо	like "oo" in look	[oh]
уу	like "oo" in moolah	[uh]

Vowels	*Approximate pronunciation*	*Phonetic transcription*
ЭЭ	like "e" in slow pronunciation of bed	[eh]
ӨӨ	like "i" in slow pronunciation of bird	[öh]
ҮҮ	like "u" in rule	[üh]
ИЙ	like "ee" in teen	[ee]

Diphthongs

ай	like "i" in like	[ai]
ой	like "oy" in boy	[oi]
уй	approx. like "ooey" in hooey	[ui]
эй	like "ay" in say	[ei]
үй	like "uoy" in buoy [boo-e]	[üi]

Vowels

Each vowel has only one sound. The pronunciation of Mongolian vowels is much simpler than the pronunciation of vowels in English.

The Mongolian vowel sounds are:

а	[a]	The sound of "a" in car
э	[e]	The sound of "a" in Amy
и	[i]	The sound of "ea" in eagle
о	[o]	The sound of "aw" in saw
у	[u]	The sound of "u" in beautiful
ө	[ö]	The sound of "e" in herd
Ү	[ü]	The sound of "u" in duty

These seven vowels are considered the basic vowels. All vowels are divided into two groups:

Masculine vowels: a, o, u, ya, yo, yu, y
Feminine vowels: e, i, ö, ü, ye, yü

The difference between masculine and feminine vowels is that masculine vowels are pronounced with the velar (back) part of the tongue, whereas feminine vowels are pronounced with the front part of the tongue. According to the rule of vowel harmony, the presence of two types of vowels, i.e. masculine and feminine, in the same word is unacceptable.

Words may be masculine or feminine, depending on which vocality is contained in the root. To the root are added word-forming suffixes or postfixes with different (basically, four) varieties of vowels. For example,

1. suffix denoting "from": -aas, -ees, -oos, -uus
2. suffix denoting "with": -tai, -tei, -toi
3. suffix denoting "by (whom)" or "by (what)": -aar, -eer, -oor, -öör etc.

The long vowels aa, ee, oo, uu, ii, öö, üü are pronounced longer than regular vowels. (In this book they are given as [ah, eh, oh, uh, ee, öh, üh].) These "long" vowels are not necessarily present in every Mongolian word; on the other hand, there may be a series of long vowels in one word. For example,

авдар [av-dar] chest (*storage*)
    This word has no long vowels, but the first "a" is pronounced longer than the second "a".

бороо [bo-rOH] rain
    This word contains just one long vowel, which is pronounced longer than the short "o".

ааруул [AH-rUHl] dried milk curd
    Both the double aa and uu are pronounced long.

Diphthongs

A diphthong is two vowels which combine to produce a single distinct sound, which acts as a single unit. Notice that the second vowel of the diphthong is always **i**. In modern Mongolian, we are concerned with five diphthongs, which should be memorized.

ай	[ai]	The sound of "a" in **bag**
эй	[ei]	The sound of "a" in **bake**
ой	[oi]	The sound of "o" in **oil**
уй	[ui]	The sound of "ooey" in **phooey**
үй	[üi]	The sound of "ui" in **suite**

Another four supplementary vowels start with a "y" sound. They may combine with other vowels to form long vowels and diphthongs:

я	[ya]	The sound of "ya" in **yahoo**
е	[ye]	The sound of "ye" in **yes**
ё	[yo]	The sound of "ya" in **yawn**
ю	[yu]	The sound of **you**

Consonants

In Mongolian there are twenty hard consonants plus their soft variants. A feature of Mongolian is that one consonant has only one pronunciation.

Mongolian consonants are identical or very similar to their English counterparts:

б as b	**в** as v	**д** as d	**г** as g in **get**
з as z	**к** as k	**л** as l	**ж** as j in **jet**
м as m	**н** as n	**п** as p	**р** as r
с as s	**т** as t	**ф** as f	

Mongolian has more consonants than English, and some of them are written in English transcription through a combination of two or more characters:

х as kh   **ц** as ts   **ч** as ch   **ш** as sh   **щ** as sch (rare)

Special attention must be paid to the pronunciation of "kh", which is similar to "h" in **have** but Mongolians pronounce it gutturally (like the "ch" in German "Ba**ch**").

Signs

There are two signs in Mongolian to indicate hard and soft consonants. The hard sign is written between consonants and vowels as a separator. E.g.,

авья   [av'ya] let's take

The soft sign softens the previous consonant. This fact is reflected orthographically by the addition of "i" after the consonant. Note particularly that whereas и "i" is a full vowel and thus is capable of forming a syllable, the soft sign designated by "i" is incapable of forming a syllable and is pronounced silently. E.g.,

ам	[am] mouth	**амь** [ami]	life
уул	[uhl] mountain	**ууль** [UHli]	owl

This difference in hardness or softness may differentiate meanings.

Stress

Word stress in Mongolian normally falls on the first syllable of a word if it contains only short vowels (although borrowed words may retain their original stress). Short vowels in the subsequent syllables take on an indistinct quality, like the "e" in the English word "the". If a word contains a long vowel (aa, ee, oo, uu, ii, öö, üü) or diphthong, however, the stress is displaced to that syllable. When a word contains more than one long vowel or diphthong, the penultimate one receives the stress. Finally, a particle added to the end of a sentence may take the stress from a preceding word.

The vowels of stressed, non-initial syllables are capitalized: da-vAH "Monday", sho-ka-lAHd "chocolate", cha-dakh chi-nEH-gEHr "if possible", sain bain UH "How are you?"

BASIC MONGOLIAN GRAMMAR

The sentence structure of Mongolian is totally different from that of English. In Mongolian, word order in a sentence is subject-object-verb.

I'll go to the city [lit., I city will go].
  Би хот руу явна.
  [bi khot ruh yav-na]

This order is preserved in interrogative sentences as well as in sentences with negatives. In an interrogative sentence, the interrogative particle comes at the end of the sentence. Interrogative particles are ...**уу** [uh], ...**үү** [üh], ... **вэ** [ve], ...**бэ** [be], ...**юу** [yuh], ...**юү** [yüh].

Shall I go to the city? (lit., I city go will?)
  Би хот руу явах **уу**?
  [bi khot ruh ya-vakh **uh**]

When are you coming?
  Чи хэзээ ирэхвэ?
  [ch khe-zEH I-rekh **ve**]

Is it a book?
  Энэ ном мөн **үү**?
  [e-ne nom mön **üh**]

Interrogative words include:

Who?
  Хэн?
  [khen]

What?
   Юу?
   [yuh]

Where?
   Хаана?
   [khAH-na]

Why?
   Яагаад?
   [yAH-gAHd]

How?
   Яаж?
   [yAHj]

How long?
   Хир удаан?
   [khir u-dAHn]

Which?
   Аль?
   [ali]

When?
   Хэзээ?
   [khe-zEH]

Where (from)?
   Хаанаас?
   [khAH-nAHs]

How many?
   Хэдэн?
   [khe-den]

How much?
   Хичнээн?
   [khich-nEHn]

Here we see that the word order is subject-interrogative word-verb-interrogative particle.

What is your name? (lit., your name what is?)
　　Таны нэр **хэн бэ?**
　　[ta-ny ner khen be]

What is it?
　　Энэ **юу вэ?**
　　[e-ne yUH ve]

When are you coming? (lit., you when coming is?)
　　Та **хэзээ** ирэх **вэ?**
　　[ta khe-zEH I-rekh ve]

Where are you **from**?
　　Та **хаанаас** ирсэн **вэ?**
　　[ta khAH-nAHs ir-sen be]

According to the rules of vowel harmony, the interrogative particle юу [yUH] is used after masculine verbs, whereas юу [yÜH] follows the feminine.

Negative sentence

Two main words are used to express the negative: "bish" and "ügüi". To make a sentence negative, simply put the word "bish" after the verb.

He is not my father
　　Энэ миний аав **биш**
　　[e-ne mi-nii ahv bish]

No, not
　　Үгүй
　　[ü-güi]

The element "-güi" is added to the verb.

I won't read this book
    Би энэ номыг уншихгүй
    [bi e-ne no-myg un-shikh-güi]

Nouns and Possessives

There are no indefinite ("a", "an") or definite ("the") arti-
cles in Mongolian. For the article "a", нэг [neg] "one"
may be used.

Possessive means that one noun modifies or possesses
another noun. In Mongolian, possessives are formed with
the suffixes -ийн [EEn], -ын [yn] (see vowel harmony)

father's book
    аавын ном
    [AH-vyn nom]

mother's photo
    ээжийн зураг
    [EH-jEEn zu-rag]

The possessives answer the question хэний [khe-nEE]
"whose"?

The Mongolian noun has seven cases.

1. who? хэн? [khen]
        brother   ах [akh]
        sister   эгч [egch]
2. whose? хэний? [khe-nEE]
        brother's   ахын [akh-yn]
        sister's   эгчийн [egch-EEn]
3. to whom? хэнд? [khend]
        to brother   ахад [akh-ad]
        to sister   эгчид [egch-id]

4. whom? **хэнийг?** [khen-EEg]
    brother   а**х**ыг [akh-yg]
    sister   эгчийг [egch-EEg]

5. from whom? **хэнээс?** [khen-EHs]
    from brother   а**х**аас [akh-AHs]
    from sister   эгчээс [egch-EHs]

6. by whom? **хэнээр?** [khen-EHr]
    by brother   а**х**аар [akh-AHr]
    by sister   эгчээр [egch-EHr]

7. with whom? **хэнтэй?** [khen-tei]
    with brother   а**х**тай [akh-tai]
    with sister   эгчтэй [egch-tei]

Plural

A singular noun is made plural by adding the particle **нар** [nar]. This type of plural form is characteristic of people and their jobs.

brothers   а**х** **нар** [akh nar]
doctors   эмч **нар** [emch nar]

When one should use the suffix **-ууд** [uhd], **-д** [d] or **-с** [s] to pluralize a noun has to be learned as there is no rule of thumb governing their usage.

names   нэр**с** [ners]
guests   зочи**д** [zo-chid]
books   номн**ууд** [nom-(n)*UHd]

*A hidden "n" appears with the suffix.

Verbs

In this phrasebook and dictionary all verbs are given in their infinitive form, which means the suffix **-х** [kh] is added to the stem of the verb. The concept of personal conjugational endings does not exist in Mongolian.

Tense in Mongolian

Present   I'm playing
           Би тоглож байна
           [bi tog-loj bain]

The word **байна** [bain] is added at the end of a sentence.

Present   I have played
perfect   Би тоглож байсан
           [bi tog-loj bai-san]

The word **байсан** [bai-san] is added at the end of a sentence.

Past   I played
           Би тоглосон
           [bi tog-lo-son]

Four types of suffixes are used to form the past tense:

- **-лаа** [lah] is added after a feminine word and **-лээ** [leh] follows a masculine word.

- **-сан** [san], **-сэн** [sen], **-сон** [son], **-сөн** [sön] follow the rules of vowel harmony.

- **-в** [v] is added to all genders.

- **-жээ** [jeh] or **-чээ** [cheh] is added to the stem of the verbs when the conversation is about third person.

Future   I will read a book.
           Би ном уншіх болно.
           [bi nom un-shikh bolno] *or*
           Би ном уншина.
           [bi nom un-shi-na]

The future tense is formed with the help of the auxiliary word **болно** [bolno] or by adding the suffix **-на** [na], **-но** [no], **-нэ** [ne], **-нө** [nö] to the verb stem.

Gender

Grammatical gender in Mongolian is the most important thing to know about a noun. Every word must be either: masculine or feminine.

The vowels **a** [a], **o** [o], **y** [u], **ы** [y], **ë** [yo], **ю** [yu], **я** [ya] are masculine vowels, and any word which contains these vowels is also masculine. On the other hand, the vowels **э** [e], **γ** [ü], **θ** [ö], **e** [ye] are feminine vowels, and any word which contains these vowels is also feminine. The **и** [i] is neutral and can occur with either gender of vowels.

The existence in Mongolian of a mixture of masculine and feminine vowels in one word is not possible. Words try to preserve their gender, something which is called **vowel harmony**. Therefore, the word suffixes that are so common in Mongolian usually have four different forms, for example: san, sen, son, sön

    av+san [took]
    ir+sen [came]
    sons+son [listened]
    ög+sön [gave]

If the names of people or places consist of two names, these words are often written together, in which case they may contain a mixture of both genders. E.g.

Энхбат [enkh-bat] enkh is translated as peace; bat is strong

Θвөрхангай [ö-vör-khan-gai] name of an *aimag*

Pronouns

Pronouns in Mongolian and English differ principally in that there is only one word in Mongolian for "he", "she" and "it", and that there is both a plain and honorific form for "you", **чи** [chi] and **та** [ta], respectively. Mongolians would call their parents, teachers or older people та, never чи. Also note that there is a plural form for you: та нар [ta nar].

I	first person, singular **би** [bi]
you	second person, singular, non-honorific **чи** [chi]
you	second person, singular, honorific **та** [ta]
he/she/it	third person or thing, singular **тэр** [ter]
we	first person, plural **бид нар** [bid nar]
you	second person, plural **та нар** [ta nar]
they	third person or thing, plural **тэд нар** [ted nar]

Declension of pronouns

I, me	**би** [bi]		
	my	миний	[mi-nEE]
	me	надад	[na-dad]
you	**чи** [chi]		
	your	чиний	[chi-nEE]
	(to) you	чамд	[chamd]
you	**та** [ta] *(deferential)*		
	your	таны	[ta-ny]
	(to) you	танд	[tand]

he		
she	тэр	[ter]
it		

	his		
	her	түүний	[tÜH-nEE]
	its		

		him		
		her	түүнд	[tÜH-nd]
		it		

we	бид	[bid]	
	our	бидний	[bid-nEE]
		us	бидэнд [bi-dend]

you	та нар	[ta nar] *(plural)*	
	your	та нарын	[ta na-ryn]
		you	та нарт [ta nart]

they	тэд	[ted]	
	their	тэдний	[ted-nEE]
		them	тэдэнд [te-dend]

Adjectives

Adjectives in Mongolian are invariable and are always placed before the noun. For example:

red flower
   улаан цэцэг
   [u-lAHn tsetseg]

I saw a **red** flower
   Би **улаан** цэцэг харсан
   [bi u-lAHn tse-tseg khar-san]
(compare: I red flower saw)

ABBREVIATIONS

Parts of speech and other relevant terms

adj.	adjective
adv.	adverb
art.	article
aux.	auxiliary verb
coll.	colloquial
conj.	conjunction
fam.	familiar
for.	formal
interj.	interjection
leg.	legal
med.	medical
n.	noun
num.	numeral *(cardinal)*
ord.	ordinal number
polit.	political
prep.	preposition
pron.	pronoun
sing.	singular
v.	verb
sth.	something
s.o.	someone

STRUCTURE OF DICTIONARY ENTRIES

A number of points should be made regarding the structure of dictionary entries in the present book.

In the English-Mongolian section, entries are listed alphabetically from A to Z; in the Mongolian-English section, alphabetical entries go from А to Я.

Typical entries from, respectively, the Mongolian-English and English-Mongolian sections of the book are as follows and will serve to illustrate the structure of entries.

бензин [ben-zin] *n.* gas *(for motor vehicles)*
ounce *n.* унц [unts] *(= 28.35 g)*

Here it should be noted that headwords are denoted by boldface text. Phonetic transcription of Mongolian words is contained in square brackets. The part of speech (n., v., adj., adv., etc) is given in italics. This is followed by the definition of the headword, together with any additional explanatory information in parentheses.

There are occasions when a single English or Mongolian word has its equivalent in the other language as two words. For example,

outer space *n.* сансар [san-sar]
энх тайван [enkh tai-van] *n.* peace

If a Mongolian rendering has multiple equivalents for an English word, they are separated by commas, e.g. **hear** *v.* сонсох [son-sokh], чагнах [chag-nakh].

If a word in one language has two quite distinct meanings in the second language, this is reflected by numbered entries. Thus,

iron *n.* 1. ИНДҮҮ [in-dÜH] *(appliance)* 2. төмөр [tö-mör] *(metal)*
баяр [ba-yar] *n.* 1. joy 2. holiday

If a word in one language may have its equivalents in two quite separate parts of speech in the second language, this is reflected by an indication of the appropriate part of speech. For example,

land *n.* газар [ga-zar]; *v.* газардах [ga-zar-dakh]

Colloquial, everyday expressions are capitalized and denoted by "*coll.*" Thus,

Help! *coll.* Туслаач! [tus-lAHch]

MONGOLIAN-ENGLISH DICTIONARY

А

аав [ahv] *n.* dad, father
аалз [ahlz] *n.* spider
аваар [a-vAHr] *n.* accident
авах [a-vakh] *v.* 1. to have 2. to take
авга [av-ga] *n.* 1. uncle 2. aunt *(on father's side)*
авгай [av-gai] *n.* 1. old lady 2. wife
авдар [av-dar] *n.* trunk *(article of luggage)*
авиа [a-via] *n.* sound
авирах [a-vi-rakh] *v.* to climb
аварга [a-var-ga] *n.* champion
аврах [av-rakh] *v.* to save *(someone's life)*
автобус [av-to-bUHs] *n.* bus
автомат [av-to-maht] *adj.* automatic
авчрах [avch-rakh] *v.* to bring
агаар [a-gAHr] *n.* air
агааржуулагч [a-gAHr-jUH-lagch] *n.* air conditioner
агуй [a-gui] *n.* cave
агуу [a-gUH] *adj.* great
агуулга [a-gUHl-ga] *n.* contents
адал явдал [a-dal yav-dal] *n.* adventure
адил [a-dil] *adj.* same
адилхан байх [a-dil-khan baikh] *v.* look like
адуу [a-dUH] *n.* horse *(generic term)*
ажиглах [a-jig-lakh] *v.* to observe
аж үйлдвэр [aj üild-ver] *n.* industry
ажил [a-jil] *n.* work, job
ажиллах [a-jil-lakh] *v.* to work
ажилтан [a-jil-tan] *n.* employee
ажил эрхлэлт [a-jil erkh-lelt] *n.* employment
аз [az] *n.* luck
айдас [ai-das] *n.* fear
айл гэр [ail ger] *n.* family
айлгах [ail-gakh] *v.* to scare

айлчин [ail-chin] *n.* guest, visitor

аймаг [ai-mag] *n. aimag (largest administrative division of Mongolia)*

аймшигтай [aim-shig-tai] *adj.* terrible, awful, scary

айраг [ai-rag] *n. airag (drink made from fermented mare's milk)*

айх [aikh] *v.* to be afraid

алах [a-lakh] *v.* to kill

албан [al-ban] *adj.* official

алдаа [al-dAH] *n.* mistake

алдар [al-dar] *n.* reputation, fame

алдарт [al-dart] *adj.* famous

аливаа [a-li-vAH] *pron., adj.* any, every

алим [a-lim] *n.* apple

алмааз [al-mAHz] *n.* diamond

алс [als] *adv.* far

алт [alt] *n.* gold

алтан [al-tan] *adj.* golden

алт мөнгөн эдлэл [alt mön-gön ed-lel] *n.* jewelry

алхах [al-khakh] *v.* to walk

аль [ali] *pron.* which

ам [am] *n.* mouth

амаргүй [a-mar-güi] *adj.* difficult, not easy, hard

амархан [a-mar-khan] *adj.* easy

амгалан [am-ga-lan] *adj.* peaceful

амжилт [am-jilt] *n.* success

амлах [am-lakh] *v.* to promise

амны алчуур [am-ny al-chUHr] *n.* napkin

амраг [am-rag] *n.* sweetheart, lover

амрах [am-rakh] *v.* to rest

амсах [am-sakh] *v.* to taste

амт [amt] *n.* taste

амтат гуа [am-tat guah] *n.* melon

амттай [amt-tai] *adj.* delicious, tasty

амттан [amt-tan] *n.* dessert

амьд [amid] *adj.* alive

амьдрал [amid-ral] *n.* life

амьдрах [amid-rakh] *v.* to live

амьтан [ami-tan] *n.* animal

анагаах [a-na-gAHkh] *v.* to treat *(disease or illness)*

анги [an-gi] *n.* class, classroom
ангилах [an-gi-lakh] *v.* to classify
анхаарал [an-khAH-ral] *n.* attention
анхаарах [an-khAH-rakh] *v.* to pay attention
анхааруулах [an-khAH-rUH-lakh] *v.* to caution
ан хийх [an khEEkh] *v.* to hunt
анчин [an-chin] *n.* hunter
арав [a-rav] *num.* ten
арал [a-ral] *n.* island
ард [ard] *n.* the people
ард [ard] *adv.* behind
ардчилал [ard-chi-lal] *n.* democracy
архи [ar-khi] *n.* alcohol; vodka
арьс [aris] *n.* skin
асаагуур [a-sAH-gUHr] *n.* cigarette lighter
асаах [a-sAHkh] *v.* to turn on
асуулт [a-sUHlt] *n.* question
асуух [as-UHkh] *v.* to ask
ах [akh] *n.* brother *(older)*
ахмад [akh-mad] *n.* the oldest, elderly *(of people)*
ач хүү [ach khÜH] *n.* grandson
ач охин [ach o-khin] *n.* granddaughter
ачаа [a-chAH] *n.* baggage, luggage
ачааны машин [a-chAH-ny ma-shin] *n.* truck
ашиг [a-shig] *n.* profit, gain
ашиггүй [a-shig-güi] *adj.* useless
ашигтай [a-shig-tai] *adj.* useful
аюул [a-yUHl] *n.* danger
аюултai [a-yUHl-tai] *adj.* dangerous
аяга [aya-ga] *n.* cup, bowl
аялал [aya-lal] *n.* tour
аялга [a-yal-ga] *n.* accent *(in speaking)*

Б

ба [ba] *conj.* and
баасан [bAH-san] *n.* Friday
баг [bag] *n.* mask
бага [ba-ga] *adj.* small, little

багаж [ba-gaj] *n.* tool
багачууд [ba-ga-chUHd] *n.* kids
багш [bagsh] *n.* teacher
байгаль [bai-gali] *n.* nature *(natural world)*
байгаль орчин [bai-gali or-chin] *n.* environment
байгуулга [bai-gUHl-ga] *n.* organization
байдал [bai-dal] *n.* situation
байнга [bain-ga] *adv.* often
байр [bair] *n.* 1. apartment 2. position *(job)*
байршил [bair-shil] *n.* location
байх [baikh] *v.* to be
байцаа [bai-tsAH] *n.* cabbage
байшин [bai-shin] *n.* building
бал [bal] *n.* honey
баллах [bal-lakh] *v.* to erase
баллуур [bal-lUHr] *n.* eraser
бал сар [bal sar] *n.* honeymoon
банан [ba-nAHn] *n.* banana
банк [bank] *n.* bank
бар [bar] *n.* tiger
бар [bahr] *n.* bar *(serving alcoholic drinks)*
бараа [ba-rAH] *n.* goods, wares
бараг [ba-rag] *adv.* almost
барагцаалбал [ba-rag-tsAHl-bal] *adj.* approximately
баримт [ba-rimt] *n.* document
барих [ba-rikh] *v.* 1. to build 2. to catch
баруун [ba-rUHn] *n., adj.* 1. west 2. right *(direction)*
бас [bas] *adv.* too, and
бат [bat] *adj.* sturdy
баталгаа [ba-tal-gAH] *n.* guarantee
батламж [bat-lakmj] *n.* confirmation
батлах [bat-lakh] *v.* to prove, confirm
бахархах [ba-khar-khakh] *v.* to be proud
баялаг [ba-ya-lag] *n.* wealth
баян [ba-yan] *adj.* rich
баяр [ba-yar] *n.* joy, happiness
баяр хүргэх [ba-yar khür-gekh] *v.* to congratulate
Баярлалаа [ba-yar-la-lAH] *coll.* Thank you
баярлах [ba-yar-lakh] *v.* 1. to be glad 2. to celebrate

баяртай [ba-yar-tai] *n.* 1. good-bye 2. *adj.* cheerful, happy

баярын өдөр [ba-ya-ryn ö-dör] *n.* holiday

бензин [ben-zin] *n.* gas *(for motor vehicles)*

би [bi] *pron.* I, me

би өөрөө [bi ÖH-röh] *pron.* myself

бид [bid] *pron.* we

бие [bi-ye] *n.* body *(human)*

биеийн байцаалт [bi-ye-EEn bai-tsAHlt] *n.* identity card

битгий [bit-gEE] *coll.* do not, not

бифштекс [bif-shteks] *n.* beefsteak

бичиг [bi-chig] *n.* 1. script 2. handwriting 3. document

бичих [bi-chikh] *v.* to write

бичээч [bi-chEHch] *n.* typist

биш [bish] *adv.* no, not

бишрэх [bish-rekh] *v.* to adore

бодлого [bod-lo-go] *n.* problem *(mathematical)*

бодох [bo-dokh] *v.* to solve

болгоомжтой [bol-gOHmj-toi] *coll.* Be careful!

болзоо [bol-zOH] *n.* date *(meeting)*

болзошгүй [bol-zosh-gui] *adv.* probably, might, could

боловсрол [bo-lovs-rol] *n.* education

боловч [bo-lovch] *conj.* although

бололцоотой [bo-lol-tsOH-toi] *adj.* available

боломж [bo-lomj] *n.* opportunity, chance

боломжтой [bo-lomj-toi] *adj.* possible

боломжгүй [bo-lomj-güi] *adj.* impossible

болох [bo-lokh] *v.* to be, become

боодол [bOH-dol] *n.* package

бороо [bo-rOH] *n.* rain

борооны цув [bo-rOH-ny tsuv] *n.* raincoat

босох [bo-sokh] *v.* 1. to get up 2. to stand up

бохир [bo-khir] *adj.* dirty

бохь [bokhi] *n.* gum *(chewing)*

бөгж [bögj] *n.* ring *(worn on finger)*

бөмбөг [böm-bög] *n.* ball

бугуйвч [bu-guivch] *n.* bracelet

будаа [bu-dAH] *n.* rice

будаг [bu-dag] *n.* paint

булан [bu-lan] *n.* corner
буруу [bu-rUH] *adj.* wrong, incorrect
буруугүй [bu-rUH-güi] *adj.* innocent
буруутай [bu-rUH-tai] *adj.* guilty
бурхан [bur-khan] *n.* God
буу [buh] *n.* gun
буудал [bUH-dal] *n.* hotel
буурал [bUH-ral] *adj.* gray
буцаах [bu-tsAHkh] *v.* to return
буцаж ирэх [bu-tsaj i-rekh] *v.* to return, come back
буцаж явах [bu-tsaj ya-vakh] *v.* to go back
буцлах [buts-lakh] *v.* to boil
буюу [bu-yUH] *conj.* or
бүгд [bügd] *adv.* all *(together)*
бүдүүн [bü-dÜHn] *adj.* fat
бүжиглэх [bü-jig-lekh] *v.* to dance
бүртгэл [bürt-gel] *n.* register
бүс [büs] *n.* belt
бүсгүй [büs-güi] *n.* lady, woman
бүтэц [bü-tets] *n.* structure
бүтээгдэхүүн [bü-tEHg-de-khÜHn] *n.* product
бэлтгэл [belt-gel] *n.* preparation
бэлтгэх [belt-gekh] *v.* to prepare
бэлэг [be-leg] *n.* gift, present
бэлэн болох [be-len bo-lokh] *adj.* ready
бэр [ber] *n.* daughter-in-law
бэрхшээл [berkh-shEHl] *n.* difficulty, hardship
бээлий [bEH-lEE] *n.* glove(s)
бялуу [bya-lUH] *n.* cake
бямба [byam-ba] *n.* Saturday
бяслаг [byas-lag] *n.* cheese
бяцхан [byats-khan] *adj.* little

В

ваар [vahr] *n.* vase
вааран эдлэл [vah-ran ed-lel] *n.* ceramics
вагон [va-gohn] *n.* railroad car
вакцин [vakt-sin] *n.* vaccine

валют [va-lyut] *n.* currency
ванн [vann] *n.* bathtub
виз [viz] *n.* visa
витамин [vi-ta-mEEn] *n.* vitamin
вокзал [vok-zAHl] *n.* railroad station
волейбол [volei-bOHl] *n.* volleyball

Г

гаа [gah] *n.* mint *(candy)*
гааль [gAHli] *n.* customs *(on the border)*
гадаа [ga-dAH] *n.* outside
гадаа гарах [ga-dAH ga-rakh] *v.* to go out
гадаад [ga-dAHd] *adj.* foreign, overseas
гадна [gad-na] *prep.* besides, except
газар [ga-zar] *n.* ground, land
газар хөдлөл [ga-zar khöd-löl] *n.* earthquake
газардах [ga-zar-dakh] *v.* to land
газрын зураг [gaz-ryn zu-rag] *n.* map
гайхалтай [gai-khal-tai] *adj.* amazing
гал [gal] *n.* fire
галын өрөө [ga-lyn ö-rÖH] *n.* kitchen
гамтai [gam-tai] *adj.* economical
ганц [gants] *adj.* alone
ганц бие [gants biye] *adj.* single
ганган [gan-gan] *adj.* elegant
гар [gar] *n.* arm *(body part)*
гарын үсэг [ga-ryn ü-seg] *n.* signature
гарах [ga-rah] *v.* to go out
гахай [ga-khai] *n.* pig
гахайн мах [ga-khain makh] *n.* pork
говь [govi] *n.* Gobi desert
гоё [go-yo] *adj.* beautiful
гол [gol] 1. *n.* river 2. *adj.* main
гомдол гарах [gom-dol gar-gakh] *v.* to complain
гомдоох [gom-dOHkh] *v.* to insult
гоо сайхан [goh sai-khan] *n.* beauty
граж [graj] *n.* garage
гуай [guai] *adj., n.* Mr., Mrs., Miss, Ms., Madam, Sir

гудамж [gu-damj] *n.* street
гуниг [gu-nig] *n.* sadness
гунигтай [gu-nig-tai] *adj.* sad
гурав [gu-rav] *num.* three
гуравдугаар [gu-rav-dug-AHr] *ord.* third
гурил [gu-ril] *n.* flour
гутал [gu-tal] *n.* shoe
гуч [guch] *num.* thirty
гүзээлзгэнэ [gu-zEHlz-gen] *n.* strawberry
гүйх [gui-kh] *v.* to run
гүүр [gühr] *n.* bridge
гэдэс [ge-des] *n.* stomach
гэмтэх [gem-tekh] *v.* to get injured
гэмших [gem-shikh] *v.* to be sorry, regret
гэнэт [ge-net] *adv.* suddenly
гэр [ger] *n.* ger *(Mongolian-style circular dwelling)*
гэр [ger] *n.* home
гэргий [ger-gEE] *n.* wife
гэрлэх [ger-lekh] *v.* to marry
гэрлэсэн [ger-le-sen] *adj.* married
гэрлээгүй [ger-lEH-gui] *adj.* unmarried, single
гэрэл [ge-rel] *n.* light
гэрээ [ge-rEH] *n.* contract
гээх [gEHkh] *v.* to lose

Д

даалгавар [dAHl-ga-var] *n.* task, assignment
даам [dAHm] *n.* checkers
даарах [dAH-rakh] *v.* to be cold
даатгал [dAHt-gal] *n.* insurance
даатгах [dAHt-gakh] *v.* to insure
даваа [da-vAH] *n.* Monday
давс [davs] *n.* salt
давтах [dav-takh] *v.* to practice, repeat
давуу тал [da-vUH tal] *n.* advantage
дагах [da-gakh] *v.* to follow
дадах [da-dakh] *v.* to get used to
дайн [dain] *n.* war

дал [dal] *num.* seventy

далай [da-lai] *n.* sea

дамжуулах [dam-jUH-lakh] *v.* to pass

дандаа [dan-dAH] *adv.* always

дараа [da-rAH] *adv.* 1. next time, later 2. after

дарга [dar-ga] *n.* chairman, chairperson

дарс [dars] *n.* wine

дасгал [das-gal] *n.* exercise

дахин [da-khin] *adv.* again

доктор [dok-tor] *n.* doctor

долдугаар [dol-du-gAHr] *ord.* seventh

долоо [do-lOH] *num.* seven

долоо хоног [do-lOH kho-nog] *n.* week

домог [do-mog] *n.* tale

доод [dOHd] *adj.* lower, bottom

доод давхар [dOHd gav-khar] *adj.* downstairs

доор [dohr] *prep.* under

доор нь [dohr ni] *adv.* underneath

дорно [dor-no] *adj.* east, eastern

дотно [dot-no] *adj.* close *(friend)*

дотоод [do-tOHd] *adj.* internal, inner

дотор [do-tor] *adj.* inside; *prep.* in

дөрөв [dö-röv] *num.* four

дөрөвдүгээр [dö-röv-dü-gEHr] *ord.* fourth

дөрөө [dö-rÖH] *n.* stirrups

дөч [döch] *num.* forty

дугаар [du-gAHr] *n.* number

-дугаар [du-gAHr] *n.* suffix for ordinal number

дугтуй [dug-tui] *n.* envelope

дугуй [du-gui] *n.* bicycle

дуг хийх [dug khEEkh] *v.* to have a nap

дулаан [du-lAHn] *adj.* warm

дунд [dund] *adj.* 1. in the middle 2. between

дунд сургууль [dund sur-gUHli] *n.* secondary school

дундаж [dun-daj] *adj.* average

дурлах [dur-lakh] *v.* to love

дурсгал [durs-gal] *n.* 1. memory 2. souvenir

дуртай [dur-tai] *adj.* favorite

дутагдах [du-tag-dakh] *v.* to be lacking

дутуу [du-tUH] *adj., adv.* less

дуу [duh] *n.* song
дуу чимээ [duh chi-mEH] *n.* noise
дуулах [dUH-lakh] *v.* to sing
дуусах [dUH-sakh] *v.* to finish
дуучин [dUH-chin] *n.* singer
дух [dukh] *n.* forehead
дүгнэлт [düg-nelt] *n.* conclusion
дүгнэх [düg-nekh] *v.* to summarize
дүн [dün] *n.* 1. result, total 2. grade *(at school)*
дүрслэн бодох [dürs-len bo-dokh] *v.* to imagine
дүрслэх урлаг [dürs-lekh ur-lag] *n.* fine arts
дүрэм [dü-rem] *n.* rule
дүү [düh] *n.* 1. brother *(younger)* 2. sister *(younger)*
дүүрэг [dÜH-reg] *n.* district
дэлгүүр [del-gÜHr] *n.* store, shop
дэр [der] *n.* pillow
дээгүүр [dEH-gÜHr] *prep.* over, on top of
дээд [dEHd] *adj.* upper, top
дээд давхар [dEHd dav-khar] *adj.* upstairs
дээд сургууль [dEHd sur-gUHli] *n.* institute
дээл [dEHl] *n.* deel *(traditional Mongolian outer garment)*
дээр [dEHr] *adj.* better

Е

ер [yer] *num.* ninety
ердийн [yör-dEEn] *adj.* simple
ерөнхий [yö-rön-khEE] *adj.* general
ерөнхийлөгч [yö-rön-khEE-lögch] *n.* president
ерөөл [yö-rÖHl] *n.* blessing
ертөнц [yör-tönts] *n.* world
ес [yös] *num.* nine
есдүгээр [yös-dü-gEHr] *ord.* ninth

Ё

ёроол [yo-rOHl] *n.* bottom
ёс заншил [yos zan-shil] *n.* tradition

ёсчлон [yosch-lon] *prep.* according to
ёслол [yos-lol] *n.* ceremony
ёстой [yos-toi] *aux.* must

Ж

жааз [jAHz] *n.* frame
жаахан [jAH-khan] *adj.* tiny
жар [jar] *num.* sixty
жаргал [jar-gal] *n.* happiness
живэх [ji-vekh] *v.* to sink
жигнэмэг [jig-ne-meg] *n.* cookie
жигнэх [jig-nekh] *v.* 1. to weigh 2. to steam *(food)*
жижиг [ji-jig] *adj.* little
жил [jil] *n.* year
жимс [jims] *n.* fruit
жин [jin] *n.* 1. scale 2. weight
жинхэнэ [jin-khe-ne] *adj.* real
жирэмсэн [ji-rem-sen] *adj.* pregnant
жишээ [ji-shEH] *n.* example
жолоодох [jo-lOH-dokh] *v.* to drive
жолооч [jo-lOHch] *n.* driver
жорлон [jor-lon] *n.* bathroom
журам [ju-ram] *n.* procedure
жуулчин [jUHl-chin] *n.* tourist
жуулчлал [jUHl-ch-lal] *n.* tourism
жүжиг [jü-jig] *n.* show *(theatrical)*
жүжигчин [jü-jig-chin] *n.* actor

З

за [za] *coll.* yes
заавал [zAH-val] *aux.* without fail, required
зааварчлага [zAH-varch-la-ga] *n.* instructions,
    manual, guide book
заах [zAHkh] *v.* to teach
заан [zAHn] *n.* elephant
зав [zav] *adv.* spare time

завсарлага [zav-sar-la-ga] *n.* break, recess
завь [zavi] *n.* boat
загас [za-gas] *n.* fish
зай [zai] *n.* battery *(electrical)*
зайлах [zai-lakh] *v.* to go away
залуу [za-lUH] *adj.* young
залуус [za-lUHs] *n.* young people
залхуу [zal-khUH] *adj.* lazy
зам [zam] *n.* 1. road 2. way *(means)*
заншил [zan-shil] *n.* custom, tradition
зар [zar] *n.* advertisement, ad
зараа [za-rAH] *n.* hedgehog
зардал [zar-dal] *n.* expenses, costs
зарах [za-rakh] *v.* to sell
зарим [za-rim] *adj.* some
зарлага [zar-la-ga] *n.* 1. messenger 2. outlay
зарлал [zar-lal] *n.* announcement
засгийн газар [zas-gEEn ga-zar] *n.* government
зах [zakh] *n.* 1. collar 2. edge 3. market
захиа [za-khia] *n.* letter *(mail)*
захирал [za-khi-ral] *n.* 1. director *(company)*
    2. principal *(school)*
зодоон [zo-dOHn] *n.* fight
золгох [zol-gokh] *v.* to greet each other *(in traditional*
    Mongolian way)
зоо парк [zoh park] *n.* zoo
зоог [zOHg] *n.* meal *(in restaurant)*
зоос [zohs] *n.* coin
зорилго [zo-ril-go] *n.* goal
зорчигч [zor-chigch] *n.* passenger
зорчих [zor-chikh] *v.* to travel
зохиол [zo-khiol] *n.* literature
зохиолч [zo-khiolch] *n.* writer
зохион байгуулах [zo-khion bai-gUH-lakh] *v.*
    to organize
зочин [zo-chin] *n.* guest
зөв [zöv] *adj.* right, correct
зөвлөгөө [zöv-lö-gÖH] *n.* advice
зөвхөн [zöv-khön] *adv.* only
зөвшөөрөл [zöv-shÖH-röl] *n.* permit, approval

зөөгч [zöhgch] *n.* waiter; waitress
зөөх [zÖHkh] *v.* to carry
зугаа [zu-gAH] *n.* fun
зул сарын баяр [zul sa-ryn bayar] *n.* Christmas
зун [zun] *n.* summer
зураач [zu-rAHch] *n.* artist, painter
зураг [zu-rag] *n.* painting
зурах [zu-rakh] *v.* to draw
зургаа [zu-rAH] *num.* six
зургадугаар [zur-ga-du-gAHr] *ord.* sixth
зуу [zuh] *num.* hundred
зууш [zuhsh] *n.* snack
зүрх [zürkh] *n.* heart *(of the body)*
зүүд [zühd] *n.* dream
зүүн [zühn] *n., adj.* 1. east 2. left *(direction)*
зүсэх [zü-sekh] *v.* to cut
зэвсэг [zev-seg] *n.* weapon
зэрлэг [zer-leg] *adj.* wild
зэрэг [ze-reg] *n.* degree *(educational)*
зээл [zehl] *n.* credit
зээлэх [zEH-lekh] *v.* to borrow

И

идэвхи [idev-khi] *n.* activity
идэвхижүүлэх [i-dev-khi-jÜH-lekh] *v.* to activate
идэр [i-der] *n.* youth
идэх [i-dekh] *v.* to eat
ижил [i-jil] *adj.* same
илгээмж [il-gEHmj] *n.* package
илтгэл [ilt-gel] *n.* 1. report 2. speech
илүү [i-lÜH] *adj.* extra
илүү их [i-lÜH ikh] *adj.* more
индүү [in-dÜH] *n.* iron *(appliance)*
инээд [i-nEHd] *n.* smile
инээх [i-nEHkh] *v.* to laugh
иргэн [ir-gen] *n.* citizen
ирэх [i-rekh] *v.* to come, arrive
ирээдүй [i-rEH-düi] *n.* future

иттэл [it-gel] *n.* hope
иттэх [it-gekh] *v.* to believe
их [ikh] *adj.* many, a lot
их дэлгүүр [ikh del-gÜHr] *n.* department store
их сургууль [ikh sur-gUHli] *n.* university

К

кабел [kah-bel] *n.* cable
кабин [ka-bEEn] *n.* cabin
календарь [ka-lyen-dari] *n.* calendar
карман [kar-man] *n.* pocket
кассчин [kass-chin] *n.* cashier
кассет [kas-syet] *n.* cassette
кафе [kafe] *n.* café
квитанц [kvi-tants] *n.* receipt
килограмм [ki-lo-gram] *n.* kilogram
километр [ki-lo-myetr] *n.* kilometer
кино [ki-no] *n.* movie
коллеж [kol-lehj] *n.* college
компани [kom-pAH-ni] *n.* company *(firm)*
компьютер [kom-pyUH-ter] *n.* computer
консерв [kon-serv] *n.* canned food
концерт [kon-tsert] *n.* concert
коньяк [kon-yak] *n.* cognac
корпус [kor-pus] *n.* corps *(e.g., Peace Corps)*
костюм [kos-tyum] *n.* suit
кофе [kOH-fe] *n.* coffee
купе [ku-pEH] *n.* compartment
куртка [kuhrt-ka] *n.* jacket

Л

лаа [lah] *n.* candle
лааз [lahz] *n.* can
лааз онгойлгогч [lahz on-goil-gogch] *n.* can opener
лавлах [lav-lakh] *v.* to make sure
лавлах толь [lav-lakh toli] *n.* guidebook

лам [lam] *n.* lama, Buddhist monk
лууван [lUH-van] *n.* carrot
лхагва [l-khag-va] *n.* Wednesday

M

маамуу [mAh-mUH] *n.* baby
магадгүй [ma-gad-güi] *adv.* perhaps, probably
май [mai] *coll.* here you are *(when handing sth. to s.o.)*
мал [mal] *n.* animal *(domesticated horse, cow, camel, goat, sheep)*
малгай [mal-gai] *n.* hat
малчин [mal-chin] *n.* herdsman
манаач [ma-nahch] *n.* watchman
манай [ma-nai] *adj.* our
манайх [ma-naikh] *pron.* ours
манан [ma-nan] *n.* fog
маргаан [mar-gAHn] *n.* argument
маргах [mar-gakh] *v.* to argue
маргааш [mar-gAHsh] *adv.* tomorrow
марк [mark] *n.* stamp *(postage)*
мартах [mar-takh] *v.* to forget
масло [mahs-lo] *n.* 1. oil 2. butter
мах [makh] *n.* meat
машин [ma-shin] *n.* car
маяг [ma-yag] *n.* style
миний [mi-nEE] *adj.* my
минийх [mi-nEEkh] *pron.* mine
минут [mi-nut] *n.* minute
могой [mo-goi] *n.* snake
мод [mod] *n.* tree
монгол хүн [mong-gol khün] *n.* Mongolian *(person)*
морь [mori] *n.* horse *(for riding)*
мотор [mo-tohr] *n.* engine
мөнгө [mön-gö] *n.* money
мөнгөн [mön-gön] *adj.* silver
мөнгөний ханш [mön-gö-nEE khansh] *n.* rate of exchange
мөөг [möhg] *n.* mushroom

мөс [mös] *n.* ice
мөхөөлдөс [mö-khÖHl-dös] *n.* ice cream
муж [muj] *n.* state *(administrative division)*
музей [mu-zei] *n.* museum
муу [mUH] *adj.* bad
муу зуршил [muh zur-shil] *n.* addiction
муур [mUHr] *n.* cat
муухай [mUH-khai] *adj.* 1. ugly 2. awful
мэдлэг [med-leg] *n.* knowledge
мэдрэх [med-rekh] *v.* to feel
мэдүүлэг [me-dÜH-leg] *n.* declaration
мэдүүлэх [me-dÜH-lekh] *v.* to declare
мэдээ [me-dEH] *n.* news
мэдэх [me-dekh] *v.* to know
мэлхий [mel-khEE] *n.* frog
мэндлэх [mend-lekh] *v.* to greet
мэндчилгээ [mend-chil-gEH] *n.* greeting
мэргэжил [mer-ge-jil] *n.* occupation
мэргэжилтэн [mer-ge-jil-ten] *n.* specialist
мэс засал [mes za-sal] *n.* surgery
мягмар [myag-mar] *n.* Tuesday

Н

наадам [nAH-dam] *n.* 1. game 2. festival
Наадам [nAH-dam] *n. festival celebrated on July 11
        and 12 each year*
наах [nahkh] *v.* to glue
наана [nah-na] *adv.* 1. over here 2. on this side
навч [navch] *n.* leaf
нагац [na-gats] *n.* 1. uncle *(on mother's side)* 2. aunt
        (on mother's side)
найдах [nai-dakh] *v.* to rely on, hope *(for)*
найдан хүлээх [nai-dan khü-lEHkh] *v.* expect
найдвар [naid-var] *n.* hope
найз [naiz] *n.* friend
найм [naim] *num.* eight
наймаа [nai-mah] *n.* commerce
найрамдал [nai-ram-dal] *n.* friendship
найрсаг [nair-sag] *adj.* friendly

нам [nam] *n.* party *(political)*
намар [na-mar] *n.* autumn
нар [nar] *n.* sun
наргиа [nar-gia] *n.* joke
нарны халх [nar-ny khalkh] *n.* umbrella
нарс [nars] *n.* pine
нас [nas] *n.* age
насанд хүрэгч [na-sand khü-regch] *n.* adult
настан [nas-tan] *n.* aged people
ная [naya] *num.* eighty
нийгэм [nEE-gem] *n.* society
нийлбэр [nEEl-ber] *n.* sum
нийслэл [nEEs-lel] *n.* capital *(city)*
нийт [nEEt] *adj.* total
нийтийн [nEE-teen] *adj.* public
нийтлэг [nEEt-leg] *adj.* typical
нимбэг [nim-beg] *n.* lemon
нимбэгний ундаа [nim-beg-nEE un-dAH] *n.* lemonade
нисгэгч [nis-gegch] *n.* pilot
нисэх [ni-sekh] *v.* to fly
ногоо [no-gOH] *n.* vegetable
ногоон [no-gOHn] *adj., n.* green
ноднин [nod-nin] *n.* last year
ном [nom] *n.* book
номын дэлгүүр [no-myn del-gÜHr] *n.* bookstore
номын сан [no-myn san] *n.* library
ноос [nohs] *n.* wool
нотолгоо [no-tol-gOH] *n.* proof *(evidence)*
нохой [no-khoi] *n.* dog
нөгөө [nö-gÖH] *adj., pron.* another
нөгөөдөр [nö-gÖH-dör] *n.* the day after tomorrow
нөхөр [nö-khör] *n.* husband
нөхцөл [nökh-tsöl] *n.* condition
нугас [nu-gas] *n.* duck
нулимс [nu-lims] *n.* tear *(from the eye)*
нусгай [nu-tag] *n.* 1. cold (illness) 2. runny nose
нутаг [nu-tag] *n.* homeland
нутагших [nu-tag-shikh] *v.* to adapt
нуур [nuhr] *n.* lake
нууц [nuhts] *n., adj.* secret

нүд [nüd] *n.* eye
нүдний шил [nüd-nEE shil] *n.* eyeglasses
нүүдэлчин [nÜH-del-chin] *n.* nomad
нүүх [nühkh] *v.* to move
нүүр [nühr] *n.* face
нүүрс [nührs] *n.* coal
нэвтрүүлэг [nevt-rÜH-leg] *n.* broadcast
нэг [neg] *num.* one
нэг удаа [neg u-dAH] *adv.* once
нэгдүгээр [neg-dü-gehr] *ord.* first
нэгдэл [neg-del] *n.* corporation
нэгдэх [neg-dekh] *v.* to unite
нэмэлт [ne-melt] *adj.* additional
нэмэх [ne-mekh] *v.* to add
нэр [ner] *n.* name
нэр алдар [ner al-dar] *n.* reputation
нэрлэх [ner-lekh] *v.* to call, to name
нэхий [ne-khEE] *n.* sheepskin
нээлт [nehlt] *n.* discovery
нээлт хийх [nehlt khEEkh] *v.* to discover
нээх [nehkh] *v.* to open
нягтлан бодогч [nyagt-lan bo-dogch] *n.* accountant
нялх хүүхэд [nyalkh khÜH-khed] *n.* baby
ням [nyam] *n.* Sunday
нямбай [nyam-bai] *adj.* punctual, careful

О

овог [o-vog] *n.* 1. surname, last name 2. patronymic
огноо [og-noo] *n.* date *(calendar)*
одоо [o-dOH] *adv.* now
оёх [oyokh] *v.* to sew
ой [oi] *n.* 1. forest 2. memory
ойн баяр [oin bayar] *n.* anniversary
ойлгох [oil-gokh] *v.* to understand
ойлс [oims] *n.* socks
ойролцоо [oi-rol-tsOH] *adv.* near to
ойрхон [oir-khon] *adv.* next to
ойчих [oi-chikh] *v.* to fall

олгой [ol-goi] *n.* appendix *(bodily organ)*
олгох [ol-gokh] *v.* to give
олж авах [olj a-vakh] *v.* to obtain
ололт [o-lolt] *n.* achievement
олон [o-lon] *adj.* many
олох [o-lokh] *v.* to find
онгоц [on-gots] *n.* airplane
онгоцны буудал [on-gots-ny bUH-dal] *n.* airport
онош [o-nosh] *n.* diagnosis
онцгой [onts-goi] *adj.* extraordinary
оо [oh] *n.* toothpaste
ор [or] *n.* bed
оргил [or-gil] *n.* peak *(summit)*
орлого [or-lo-go] *n.* income
орлогын татвар [or-lo-gyn tat-var] *n.* income tax
орой [o-roi] *n.* evening
оройн хоол [o-roin khohl] *n.* dinner
оройтох [o-roi-tokh] *v.* to be late
оролдох [o-rol-dokh] *v.* try
оролцох [o-rol-tsokh] *v.* to attend, to participate
оролцуулан [o-rol-tsUH-lan] *prep.* including
орон [o-ron] *n.* country
орос [o-ros] *n.* 1. Russia 2. Russian *(person)*
орох [o-rokh] *v.* to enter
орох хаалга [o-rokh khAHl-ga] *n.* entrance
орчим [or-chim] *adv.* around, about
орчин үеийн [or-chin ü-ye-EEn] *adj.* modern
орчуулагч [or-chUH-lagch] *n.* translator
орчуулах [or-chUH-lakh] *v.* to translate
орчуулга [or-chUH-ga] *n.* translation
оршуулгын газар [or-shUH-gyn ga-zar] *n.* cemetery
офицер [ofi-tser] *n.* officer
охин [o-khin] *n.* daughter
оюутан [oyUH-tan] *n.* student

Θ

өв [öv] *n.* heritage
өвгөн [öv-gön] *n.* old man

өвгөрөх [öv-gö-rökh] *v.* to get old
өвдөг [öv-dög] *n.* knee
өвөл [ö-völ] *n.* winter
өвөө [ö-vÖH] *n.* grandfather
өвөрмөц [ö-vör-möts] *adj.* specific, particular
өвс [övs] *n.* hay, grass
өвчин [öv-chin] *n.* illness, disease
өвчтөн [övch-tön] *n.* patient
өглөө [ög-lÖH] *n.* morning
өглөөний цай [ög-lÖH-nEE tsai] *n.* breakfast
өглөөгүүр [ög-lÖH-gÜHr] *adv.* in the morning
өгөөмөр [ö-gÖH-mör] *adj.* generous
өгөх [ö-gökh] *v.* to give
өгүүлбэр [ö-gÜHl-ber] *n.* sentence *(grammatical)*
өгүүллэг [ö-gÜHl-leg] *n.* story
өдөр [ö-dör] *n.* day
өдрийн хоол [öd-rEEn khohl] *n.* lunch, midday meal
өдөржин [ö-dör-jin] *adv.* during the day
өдөр тутмын [ö-dör tut-myn] *adj.* daily
өлгөх [öl-gökh] *v.* to hang
өлгүүр [öl-gÜHr] *n.* clothes-hanger
өлсөх [öl-sökh] *v.* to be hungry
өмгөөлөгч [öm-gÖH-lögch] *n.* attorney
өмд [ömd] *n.* trousers, pants
өмнө [öm-nö] *n.* south *(direction)*
өмнө (2 жилийн) [öm-nö (kho-yor ji-lEEn)] *adv.* (two years) ago
өмсөх [öm-sökh] *v.* to wear
өмч [ömch] *n.* property
өнгө [ön-gö] *n.* color
өнгөрсөн [ön-gör-sön] *n.* past
өндөг [ön-dög] *n.* egg
өндөр [ön-dör] *adj.* tall
өнөөдөр [ö-nÖH-dör] *n.* today
өнчин [ön-chin] *n., adj.* orphan
өөр [öhr] *adj.* another, different
өөрөө [ÖH-rÖH] *pron.* myself; himself; herself
өөх [öhkh] *n.* fat *(on meat)*
өргөдөл [ö-rög-döl] *n.* petition, application

өргөн [ör-gön] 1. *n.* width 2 *adj.* wide
өргөн чөлөө [ör-gön chö-lÖH] *n.* avenue
өргөө [ör-gÖH] *n.* palace
өргөст хэмх [ör-göst khemkh] *n.* cucumber
өрнө [ör-nö] *n.* west
өрөө [ö-rÖH] *n.* room *(in house)*
өртэй байх [ör-tei baikh] *v.* to owe
өрх гэр [örkh ger] *n.* family
өршөөл [ör-shÖHl] *n.* pardon, forgiveness
өсгий [ös-gEE] *n.* heel *(of one's foot)*
өсгөх [ös-gökh] *v.* to increase, raise
өсөх [ö-sökh] *v.* to grow up
өчигдөр [ö-chig-dör] *n.* yesterday

П

пальто [pali-to] *n.* coat
парламент [par-lah-ment] *n.* parliament
паспорт [pahs-port] *n.* passport
пиво [pEE-vo] *n.* beer
програм [prog-rahm] *n.* program
практик [prak-tik] *n.* practice
протокол [pro-to-kol] *n.* minutes *(of a meeting)*
профессор [pro-fes-sor] *n.* professor
пүрэв [pü-rev] *n.* Thursday

Р

радио [ra-dio] *n.* radio
размер [raz-mer] *n.* size
район [ra-ion] *n.* district
рам [ram] *n.* frame
резин [re-zin] *n.* rubber
ресторан [res-to-rAHn] *n.* restaurant
руу [ruh] *prep.* to *(toward, in the direction of)*
рүү [rüh] same as **руу**

C

саад болох [sahd bo-lokh] *v.* to disturb, to bother
сав [sav] *n.* container
саван [sa-van] *n.* soap
сагс [sags] *n.* basket
садан [sa-dan] *n.* relative, relation
сайд [said] *n.* minister
сайжруулах [saij-rUH-lakh] *v.* to improve
сайн [sain] *adj.* good, nice
сайхан [sai-khan] *adj.* beautiful
салад [sa-lAHd] *n.* salad
салбар [sal-bar] *n.* branch
салхи [sal-khi] *n.* wind
салхилах [sal-khi-lakh] *v.* to blow *(as the wind)*
салхитай [sal-khi-tai] *adj.* windy
сам [sam] *n.* comb
самар [sa-mar] *n.* nut, peanut
самбар [sam-bar] *n.* blackboard
санаа [sa-nAH] *n.* idea
санаачлага [sa-nAHch-la-ga] *n.* initiative
санагдах [sa-nag-dakh] *v.* to seem
санал [sa-nal] *n.* opinion
санал болгох [sa-nal bol-gokh] *v.* to offer; to recommend
санамсаргүй [sa-nam-sar-güi] *adj.* accidental, unplanned
санах [sa-nakh] *v.* to remember
санах [sa-nakh] *v.* to miss *(s.o.)*
сандал [san-dal] *n.* chair
сансар [san-sar] *n.* outer space
сануулах [sa-nUH-lakh] *v.* to remind
сануулга [sa-nUHl-ga] *n.* caution
санхүү [san-khÜH] *n.* finance
сар [sar] *n.* 1. moon 2. month
сарлаг [sar-lag] *n.* yak
сармагчин [sar-mag-chin] *n.* monkey
сармис [sar-mis] *n.* garlic
сарнай [sar-nai] *n.* rose
сахал [sa-khal] *n.* beard

сахилга [sa-khil-ga] *n.* discipline

сая [saya] *num.* million

сая [saya] *adv.* just

саяхан [saya-khan] *adv.* recently

спирт [spirt] *n.* alcohol

согтуу [sog-tUH] *adj.* drunk

соёл [so-yol] *n.* culture

соёмбо [so-yom-bo] *n. soyombo (state emblem of Mongolia)*

солилцох [so-lil-tsokh] *v.* to exchange

солих [so-likh] *v.* to change

солонго [so-lon-go] *n.* rainbow

сонгино [son-gi-no] *n.* onion

сонгогдох [son-gog-dokh] *v.* to be chosen, elected

сонгодог [son-go-dog] *adj.* classic

сонгох [son-gokh] *v.* to choose

сонгууль [son-gUHli] *n.* election

сонин [so-nin] *n.* newspaper

сонирхол [so-nir-khol] *n.* interest

сонирхолтой [so-nir-khol-toi] *adj.* interesting

сонирхох [so-nir-khokh] *v.* to be interested in sth.

сонсох [son-sokh] *v.* to hear

сормуус [sor-mUHs] *n.* eyelash

сорох [so-rokh] *v.* to suck in

соус [sous] *n.* sauce

сохор [so-khor] *adj.* blind

сөрөг [sö-rög] *adj.* negative

сувд [suvd] *n.* pearl

сувилагч [su-vi-lagch] *n.* nurse

судалгаа [su-dal-gAH] *n.* 1. research 2. study

судлах [sud-lakh] *v.* to study

сул [sul] *adj.* weak

сулрах [sul-rakh] *v.* to weaken, become weak

сум [sum] *n. sum (small administrative division)*

сураг [su-rag] *n.* piece of news

сурагч [su-ragch] *n.* student, pupil

сурах [su-rakh] *v.* to study

сурвалжлагч [sur-balj-lagch] *n.* correspondent

сугалаа [su-ga-lAH] *n.* lottery

сургах [sur-gakh] *v.* to teach

сургууль [sur-gUHli] *n.* school
суудал [sUH-dal] *n.* seat
суут [suht] *n.* genius
суух [suhkh] *v.* to sit
сууц [suhts] *n.* apartment
сүлжээ [sül-jEH] *n.* network
сүм [süm] *n.* church, temple *(Buddhist)*
сүү [süh] *n.* milk
сүүдэр [sÜH-der] *n.* shadow
сүүл [sühl] *n.* tail
сүүлийн [sÜH-lEEn] *adj.* last
сүүмс [sühms] *n.* gravy
сүх [sükh] *n.* axe
сэлэх [se-lekh] *v.* to swim
сэргийлэгч [ser-gEE-legch] *n.* police officer
сэрүүлэг [se-rÜH-leg] *n.* alarm clock
сэрүүн [se-rÜHn] *adj.* cool
сэрэглэн [se-reg-len] *adj.* smart
сэрэх [se-rekh] *v.* to wake up
сэрээ [se-rEH] *n.* fork
сэтгүүл [set-gÜHl] *n.* magazine
сэтгэгдэл [set-geg-del] *n.* impression
сэтгэгдэл төрүүлэх [set-geg-del tö-rÜH-lekh] *v.*
    to impress
сэтгэл [set-gel] *n.* spirit
сэтгэх [set-gekh] *v.* 1. to reflect 2. to figure out
сэхээтэн [se-khEH-ten] *n.* intellectual

Т

та [ta] *pron.* you *(honorific form)*
тааз [tahz] *n.* ceiling
таалагдах [tAH-lag-dakh] *v.* to be liked
таалал [tah-lal] *n.* desire
таалах [tAH-lakh] *v.* to like
таамаг [tah-mag] *n.* guess
таарамж [tah-ramj] *n.* 1. fitness 2. harmony
таарах [tAH-rakh] *v.* to suit
таатай [tah-tai] *adj.* pleasant

таах [tahkh] *v.* to guess
тав [tav] *num.* five
таваг [ta-vag] *n.* plate
тавилга [ta-vil-ga] *n.* furniture
тавих [ta-vikh] *v.* to put
тавтай [tav-tai] *adj.* comfortable
тавь [tavi] *num.* fifty
тайван [tai-van] 1. *n.* peace 2. *adj.* quiet
тайлан [tai-lan] *v.* to report
тайлбар [tail-bar] *n.* explanation
тайлбарлагч [tail-bar-lagch] *n.* commentator
тайлбарлах [tail-bar-lakh] *v.* to explain
тайтгарах [tait-ga-rakh] *v.* to calm down
такси [tak-si] *n.* taxi
тал [tal] 1. *n.* steppe 2. *adj.* half
талархал [ta-lar-khal] *n.* appreciation
талархах [ta-lar-khakh] *v.* to be grateful, appreciate
талбай [tal-bai] *n.* area
талх [talkh] *n.* bread
тамга [tam-ga] *n.* stamp
тамхи [tam-khi] *n.* cigarette
тамхи татах [tam-khi ta-takh] *v.* to smoke
танай [ta-nai] *pron.* yours
тангараглах [tan-ga-rag-lax] *v.* to swear *(affirm)*
танил [ta-nil] 1. *n.* acquaintance 2. *adj.* familiar
танилцах [ta-nil-tsakh] *v.* to meet
танилцуулах [ta-nil-tsUH-lakh] *v.* to introduce
таних [ta-nikh] *v.* to recognize
тансаг [tan-sag] 1. *n.* luxury 2. *adj.* lovely
тарвага [tar-va-ga] *n.* marmot
тарган [tar-gan] *adj.* fat
тариа [ta-ria] *n.* 1. corn *(crop)* 2. injection, shot
тарих [ta-rikh] *v.* 1. to plant 2. to give an injection
тархи [tar-khi] *n.* brain
тасаг [ta-sag] *n.* section
тасалбар [ta-sal-bar] *n.* ticket
татвар [tat-var] *n.* tax
татгалзах [tat-gal-zakh] *v.* to refuse, to reject
тахиа [ta-khia] *n.* chicken
театр [teatr] *n.* theater

телевиз [te-le-viz] *n.* television

техник [tekh-nik] *n.* technology

тив [tiv] *n.* continent

тийм [teem] *coll.* yes

товч [tovch] *n.* button

товчоо [tov-chOH] *n.* agency, bureau

тоглолт [tog-lolt] *n.* 1. performance 2. match *(in sports)*

тоглоом [tog-lOHm] *n.* toy, game

тоглох [tog-lokh] *v.* to play

тогооч [to-gOHch] *n.* cook

тогтмол [togt-mol] *adj.* regular

тогших [tog-shikh] *v.* to knock

тодорхойлох [to-dor-khoi-lokh] *v.* to determine

тодорхойлолт [to-dor-khoi-lolt] *n.* 1. definition *(of a word)* 2. reference

тойрог [toi-rog] *n.* circle

толбо [tol-bo] *n.* spot *(blemish)*

толгой [tol-goi] *n.* head

толь [toli] *n.* mirror

том [tom] *adj.* big

тоног төхөөрөмж [to-nog tö-khOH-römj] *n.* equipment

тоо [toh] *n.* (any) number *(e.g., 58)*

тоолох [tOH-lokh] *v.* to count

тоолуур [tOH-lUHr] *n.* meter, counter

тоос [tohs] *n.* dust, dirt

тооцоо [tOH-tsOH] *n.* 1. account 2. bill *(in restaurant)*

торго [tor-go] *n.* silk

торт [tohrt] *n.* pie, cake

тохилог [to-khi-log] *adj.* convenient

тохиролцоо [to-khi-rol-tsOH] *n.* agreement

төв [töv] *n.* center

төгс [tögs] *adj.* complete

төгсгөл [tögs-göl] *n.* ending

төгсөх [tög-sökh] *v.* 1. to end, to finish 2. to graduate *(college)*

төлбөр [töl-bör] *n.* payment, fee

төлөв [tö-löv] *n.* condition

төлөө [tö-lÖH] *adv.* instead of

төлөөлөгч [tö-lÖH-lögch] *n.* delegate

төлөх [tö-lökh] *v.* to pay

төмөр [tö-mör] *n.* iron *(metal)*
төмөр зам [tö-mör zam] *n.* railroad
төмс [töms] *n.* potato
төр [tör] *n.* state *(polit.)*
төрөлх [tö-rölkh] *adj.* native
төрөх [tö-rökh] *v.* to give birth
төрсөн өдөр [tör-sön ö-dör] *n.* birthday
төсөв [tö-söv] *n.* budget
төсөл [tö-söl] *n.* project
төсөөлөл [tö-sÖH-löl] *n.* 1. imagination 2. idea
туранхай [tu-ran-khai] *adj.* thin
турах [tu-rakh] *v.* to lose weight
турш [tursh] *adv.* during
туршилт [tur-shilt] *n.* experiment
туршлага [tursh-la-ga] *n.* experience
тусгай [tus-gai] *adj.* separate
туслах [tus-lakh] *v.* to help
туулай [tUH-lai] *n.* rabbit
тухай [tu-khai] *adv.* about
тухтай [tukh-tai] *adj.* comfortable
тушаал [tu-shAHl] *n.* order
түймэр [tüi-mer] *n.* fire
түлхүүр [tül-khÜHr] *n.* key
түнш [tünsh] *n.* companion
түргэн тусламж [tür-gen tus-lamj] *n.* ambulance
түрийвч [tü-rEEvch] *n.* wallet
түүх [tühkh] *n.* history
түүхий [tÜH-khEE] *adj.* raw
түүхт [tühkht] *adj.* historical
тэг [teg] *n.* zero
тэгэлгүй яахав [te-gel-güi yAH-khav] *adv.* certainly
тэмдэглэх [tem-deg-lekh] *v.* to celebrate
тэмцэл [tem-tsel] *n.* struggle
тэмцээн [tem-tsEHn] *n.* contest, match
тэмээ [te-mEH] *n.* camel
тэнгэр [ten-ger] *n.* sky
тэнгис [ten-gis] *n.* sea
тэнцэх [ten-tsekh] *v.* to balance
тэр (эмэгтэй) [ter (e-meg-tei)] *pron.* she
тэр (эрэгтэй) [ter (e-reg-tei)] *pron.* he

тэсвэртэй [tes-ver-tei] *adj.* patient
тээвэр [tEH-ver] *n.* transportation
тээш [tehsh] *n.* luggage, baggage

У

угаах [u-gAHkh] *v.* 1. to wash 2. to do the laundry
угаалга [u-gAHl-ga] *n.* laundry
улаан [u-dAHn] *adj.* slow
удам [u-dam] *n.* lineage
удахгүй [u-dakh-güi] *adv.* soon
удирдамж [u-dir-damj] *n.* direction
удирдлага [u-dird-la-ga] *n.* management
удирдагч [u-dir-dagch] *n.* leader
уйтгар [uit-gar] *n.* boredom
улаан [u-lAHn] *adj.* red
улам их [u-lam ikh] *adv.* more
уламжлал [u-lamj-lal] *n.* tradition
улирал [u-li-ral] *n.* season
улс [uls] *n.* country, state
унагах [u-na-gakh] *v.* to drop *(down)*
унах [u-nakh] *v.* to fall *(down)*
унах (морь) [u-nakh (mori)] *v.* to ride *(a horse)*
ундаа [un-dAH] *n.* drink
унтах [un-takh] *v.* to sleep
унтлагын өрөө [unt-la-gyn ö-rÖH] *n.* bedroom
унтлагын хувцас [unt-la-gyn khuv-tsas] *n.* pajamas
унтраалга [unt-rAHl-ga] *n.* switch
унтраах [unt-rAHkh] *v.* to turn off *(light, television)*
унц [unts] *n.* ounce *(28.35 g)*
унших [un-shikh] *v.* to read
урагшаа [u-rag-shAH] *adv.* ahead
урагшлах [u-ragsh-lakh] *v.* advance
уралдаан [u-ral-dAHn] *n.* race, competition
уран зураг [u-ran zu-rag] *n.* art
ургамал [ur-ga-mal] *n.* plant *(botanical)*
ургах [ur-gakh] *v.* to grow
урд [urd] *adj.* south
уржигдар [ur-jig-dar] *n.* the day before yesterday

урҗнан [urj-nan] *n.* the year before last
урих [u-rikh] *v.* to invite
урт [urt] *adj.* long
уруул [u-rUHl] *n.* lip
урьдчилан [urid-chi-lan] *adv.* in advance
ус [us] *n.* water
усан үзэм [u-san ü-zem] *n.* grape
утаа [u-tAH] *n.* smoke
утас [u-tas] *n.* 1. thread 2. telephone
утасдах [u-tas-dakh] *v.* to phone
утга [ut-ga] *n.* meaning
уул [uhl] *n.* mountain
уулзалт [uhl-zalt] *n.* meeting
уулзах [uhl-zakh] *v.* to meet
уулзвар [uhlz-var] *n.* intersection
уур амьсгал [uhr amis-gal] *n.* climate
уурлах [uhr-lakh] *v.* to be angry
ууртai [uhr-tai] *adj.* moody
уух [uhkh] *v.* to drink
уучлах [UHch-lakh] *v.* to forgive
ухаалаг [u-khAH-lag] *adj.* clever
ухаан [u-khAHn] *n.* mind, intellect
ухаантай [u-khAHn-tai] *adj.* smart
ухамсарлах [u-kham-sar-lakh] *v.* to realize
учир [u-chir] *adv.* because

Y

үг [üg] *n.* word
үгүй [ü-güi] *adv.* no
үд [üd] *n.* noon
үдээс [ü-dEHs] *n.* lace
үдээс өмнө [ü-dEhs öm-nö] *n.* morning, A.M.
үдээс хойш [ü-dEHs khoish] *n.* afternoon, P.M.
үдэх [ü-dekh] *v.* to accompany
үдэш [ü-desh] *n.* evening
үдэшлэг [ü-desh-leg] *n.* party *(social)*
үер [ü-yer] *n.* flood
үзэг [ü-zeg] *n.* pen

үзэм [ü-zem] *n.* raisins
үзэн ядах [ü-zen ya-dakh] *v.* to hate
үзэсгэлэн [ü-zes-ge-len] *n.* exhibition
үзэх [ü-zekh] *v.* to watch
үйлдвэр [üild-ver] *n.* factory
үйлдвэрлэх [üild-ver-lekh] *v.* to produce, make
үйлчлэгч [üilch-legch] *n.* clerk
үл [ül] *prep.* not
үлдэх [ül-dekh] *v.* to remain
үндэсний [ün-des-nEE] *adj.* national
үндэстэн [ün-des-ten] *n.* nationality
үндсэн [ünd-sen] *adj.* basic
үндсэн хууль [ünd-sen khUHli] *n.* constitution
үндэс [ün-des] *n.* 1. root 2. basis
үнс [üns] *n.* ash
үнсний сав [üns-nEE sav] *n.* ashtray
үнсэх [ün-sekh] *v.* to kiss
үнэ [ü-ne] *n.* price
үнэг [ü-neg] *n.* fox
үнэмлэх [ü-nem-lekh] *n.* 1. license 2. certificate
үнэн [ü-nen] *n.* truth
үнэнч [ü-nench] *adj.* honest
үнэр [ü-ner] *n.* smell
үнэрлэх [ü-ner-lekh] *v.* 1. to sniff 2. to smell
үнэртэй ус [ü-ner-tei us] *n.* perfume
үнэртэн [ü-ner-ten] *n.* fragrance
үнэтэй [ü-ne-tei] *adj.* expensive
үнэтэй бус [ü-ne-tei bus] *adj.* inexpensive
үнэхээр [ü-ne-khEHr] *adv.* absolutely
үр [ür] *n.* seed
үр ашигтай [ür a-shig-tai] *adj.* efficient
үргэлж [ür-gelj] *adv.* always
үргэлжлэл [ür-gelj-lel] *n.* continuation
үрчлэх [ürch-lekh] *v.* to adopt
үс [üs] *n.* hair
үсчин [üs-chin] *n.* hairdresser, barber
үсэг [ü-seg] *n.* letter *(of alphabet)*
үсэглэх [ü-seg-lekh] *v.* to spell
үүд [ühd] *n.* door
үүл [ühl] *n.* cloud

үүнийх [ÜH -nEEkh] *pron.* its
үүр [ühr] *n.* nest
үүрд [ührd] *adj.* eternal
үүрэг [ÜH-reg] *n.* responsibility
үхрийн мах [ükh-rEEn makh] *n.* beef
үхэл [ü-khel] *n.* death
үхэх [ü-khekh] *v.* to die
үхэр [ü-kher] *n.* cow

Ф

факультет [fa-kuli-teht] *n.* faculty *(at a university)*
фестиваль [festi-val] *n.* festival
ферм [ferm] *n.* farm
физик [fi-zik] *n.* physics
физологи [fi-zo-lo-gi] *n.* physiology
философи [fi-la-so-fi] *n.* philosophy
фонд [fond] *n.* foundation

Х

хаалга [khAHl-ga] *n.* door
хаан [khahn] *n.* king
хаана [khAH-na] *adv.* where
хаанаас [khAH-nAHs] *adv.* from where
хаах [khahkh] *v.* to close
хаачих [khAH-chikh] *v.* to go somewhere
хаашаа [khAH-shAH] *adv.* where
хааяа [khAH-yAH] *adv.* sometimes
хавар [kha-var] *n.* spring *(season)*
хавсралт [khavs-ralt] *n.* appendix *(of a book)*
хавтас [khav-tas] *n.* 1. folder 2. binder 3. cover *(book)*
хавцал [khav-tsal] *n.* canyon
хагас [kha-gas] *adj.* half
хадам аав [kha-dàm ahv] *n.* father-in-law
хадам ээж [kha-dam ehj] *n.* mother-in-law
хадгалах [khad-ga-lakh] *v.* to save, to keep
хадгаламж [khad-ga-lamj] *n.* savings account

хазаар [kha-zAhr] *n.* halter
хайр [khair] *n.* love
хайрлах [khair-lakh] *v.* to love
хайрт [khairt] *adj.* dear, darling
хайрцаг [khair-tsag] *n.* box
хайх [khaikh] *v.* to search
хайч [khaich] *n.* scissors
халаалт [kha-lAHlt] *n.* heat
халбага [khal-ba-ga] *n.* spoon
халуун [kha-lUHn] *adj.* hot
халх [khalkh] *n. Khalkh (basic nationality in central Mongolia)*
хамаатан [kha-mAH-tan] *n.* relatives
хамаг [kha-mag] *adj.* all
хамар [kha-mar] *n.* nose
хамгаалалт [kham-gAH-lalt] *n.* protection
хамгаалах [kham-gAH-lakh] *v.* to guard, protect
хамгийн [kham-gEEn] *adj.* the most
хамт [khamt] *adv.* together
хан боргоцой [khan bor-go-tsoi] *n.* pineapple
хан хүү [khan khüh] *n.* prince
хана [kha-na] *n.* wall
хангалттай [khan-galt-tai] *adj., adv.* enough
хань [khani] *n.* spouse
хар [khar] *adj.* black
хараа [kha-rAH] *n.* sight *(vision)*
харайх [kha-raikh] *v.* to jump
харандаа [kha-ran-dAH] *n.* pencil
харанхуй [kha-ran-khui] *adj.* dark
харах [kha-rakh] *v.* to see
харин [kha-rin] *conj.* but
хариу [kha-riu] *n.* answer
хариулах [kha-riu-lakh] *v.* to reply
харих [kha-rikh] *v.* to go home
харьцаа [khari-tsAH] *n.* relation, relationship
хасах [kha-sakh] 1. *n.* minus 2. *v.* to subtract
хатуу [kha-tUH] *adj.* hard
хахууль [kha-khUHli] *n.* bribe
хацар [kha-tsar] *n.* cheek
хачин [kha-chin] *adj.* strange, funny

хашаа [kha-shAH] *n.* fence
хаяг [kha-yag] *n.* address
хаях [kha-yakh] *v.* to throw
хиам [khiam] *n.* sausage, salami
хивс [khivs] *n.* carpet
хий [khee] *n.* air
хийх [kheekh] *v.* to do, to make
хил [khil] *n.* border
хими [khi-mi] *n.* chemistry
хичнээн [khich-nEHn] *adv.* how much, how many
хичээл [khi-chEHl] *n.* lesson
хичээх [khi-chEHkh] *v.* to try
ховор [kho-vor] *adj.* rare
хог [khog] *n.* trash
ходоод [kho-dOHd] *n.* stomach
хоёр [kho-yor] *num.* two
хоёрдугаар [kho-yor-du-gAHr] *ord.* second
хождох [khoj-dokh] *v.* to lose
хойно [khoi-no] *adv.* behind
хойтон [khoi-ton] *n.* next year
хол [khol] *adv.* far
холын [kho-lyn] *adj.* distant
хонгор [khon-gor] *adj.* darling
хоног [kho-nog] *n.* twenty-four-hour period
хонх [khonkh] *n.* bell
хонь [khoni] *n.* sheep
хоол [khohl] *n.* 1. meal 2. food
хооллох [khOHl-lokh] *v.* to eat
хоолой [khOH-loi] *n.* throat
хооронд [khOH-rond] *prep.* between
хоосон [khOH-son] *adj.* empty
хориглох [kho-rig-lokh] *v.* to prohibit
хорхой [khor-khoi] *n.* insect
хорь [khori] *num.* twenty
хос [khos] *n., adj.* pair
хот [khot] *n.* city, town
хоч [khoch] *n.* nickname
хошин [kho-shin] *adj.* satirical
хөвөн [khö-vön] *n.* cotton
хөгжил [khög-jil] *n.* progress

хөгжим [khög-jim] *n.* music

хөгжимчин [khög-jim-chin] *n.* musician

хөгжүүлэх [khög-jÜH-lekh] *v.* to develop

хөгшин [khög-shin] *adj.* old

хөдөлгөөн [khö-döl-gÖHn] *n.* 1. movement 2. motion

хөдөлмөр [khö-döl-mör] *n.* labor, work

хөдөө [khö-dÖH] *n.* countryside

хөзөр [khö-zör] *n.* cards *(playing)*

хөл [khöl] *n.* leg

хөлдөх [khöl-dökh] *v.* to freeze

хөлийн хуруу [khö-lEEn khu-rUH] *n.* toe

хөлрөх [khöl-rökh] *v.* to sweat

хөлс [khöls] *n.* sweat

хөлслөх [khöls-lökh] *v.* to rent

хөмсөг [khöm-sög] *n.* eyebrow

хөнгөн [khön-gön] *adj.* light *(not heavy)*

хөнжил [khön-jil] *n.* blanket

хөө [khöh-ye] *interj.* hey

хөөмий [khÖH-mEE] *n.* throat singing

хөөрхөн [khÖHr-khön] *adj.* beautiful

хөрөх [khö-rökh] *v.* to get cold

хөрөнгө [khö-rön-gö] *n.* property

хөрш [khörsh] *n.* neighbor

хөтөлбөр [khö-töl-bör] *n.* program

хөх [khökh] 1. *n.* teat 2. *adj.* blue

хөшиг [khö-shig] *n.* curtain

хөшөө [khö-shÖH] *n.* monument

хуваах [khu-vAHkh] *v.* to divide

хувийн [khu-vEEn] *adj.* personal, private

хувцас [khuv-tsas] *n.* clothes

хувцаслах [khuv-tsas-lakh] *v.* to get dressed

хувь [khuvi] *n.* percent

хугацаа [khu-ga-tsAH] *n.* time

худал [khu-dal] *adj.* false, untrue

худал хэлэх [khu-dal khe-lekh] *v.* to lie *(to tell an untruth)*

худалдаа [khu-dal-dAH] *n.* trade, commerce

худалдан авагч [khu-dal-dan a-vagch] *n.* customer

худалдан авах [khu-dal-dan a-vakh] *v.* to buy

худалдах [khu-dal-dakh] *v.* to sell

хурал [khu-ral] *n.* meeting
хурд [khurd] *n.* speed
хурдан [khur-dan] *adj.* fast, quick
хурдлах [khurd-lakh] *v.* to accelerate
хурим [khu-rim] *n.* wedding
хуруу [khu-rUH] *n.* finger
хурц [khurst] *adj.* sharp *(cutting easily)*
хутга [khut-ga] *n.* knife
хуудас [khUH-das] *n.* page *(of a book)*
хуулах [khUH-lakh] *v.* to copy out, to write out
хуулбар [khUHl-bar] *n.* copy
хууль [khUHli] *n.* law
хууль бус [khUHli bus] *adj.* illegal
хууль ёсны [khUHli yos-ny] *adj.* legal
хуульч [khUHlich] *n.* lawyer
хуурай [khUH-rai] *adj.* dry
хуучин [khUH-chin] *adj.* old
хүзүү [khü-zÜH] *n.* neck
хүйтэн [khüi-ten] *adj.* cold
хүлээх [khü-lEHkh] *v.* to wait
хүлээн авах [khü-lEHn a-vakh] *v.* to receive
хүлээн зөвшөөрөх [khü-lEHn zöv-shÖH-rökh] *v.* to admit, accept
хүмүүс [khü-mÜHs] *n.* people
хүн [khün] *n.* person
хүнд [khünd] *adj.* heavy
хүндлэх [khünd-lekh] *n.* respect
хүнс [khüns] *n.* food
хүнсний зах [khüns-nEE zakh] *n.* food market
хүнсний зүйлс [khüns-nEE züils] *n.* grocery
хүргэн [khür-gen] *n.* son-in-law
хүргэх [khür-gekh] *v.* to deliver
хүртэл [khür-tel] *prep.* until
хүсэл [khü-sel] *n.* wish, desire
хүсэх [khü-sekh] *v.* to want
хүү [khüh] *n.* 1. son 2. boy
хүүхэд [khÜH-khed] *n.* child
хүүхэн [khÜH-khen] *n.* woman
хүч [khüch] *n.* strength
хүчинтэй [khü-chin-tei] *adj.* valid

хүчит [khü-chit] *adj.* powerful

хэвлэгч [khev-legch] *n.* printer *(machine or person)*

хэвлэх [khev-lekh] *v.* to publish

хэд(эн) [khed(en)] *adj.* some, several

хэдүгээр [khed-dü-gEHr] *adv.* which

хэдий чинээн [khe-dEE chi-nEEn] *adv.* how much

хэдийд [khe-dEEd] *adv.* when

хэзээ [khe-zEH] *adv.* when

хэзээ ч үгүй [khe-zEH ch ü-güi] *adv.* never

хэл [khel] *n.* 1. language 2. tongue

хэлзүй [khel züi] *n.* grammar

хэлмэрч [khel-merch] *n.* interpreter

хэлтэс [khel-tes] *n.* department

хэлэлцэх [khe-lel-tsekh] *v.* to discuss

хэлэх [khe-lekh] *v.* to say

хэм [khem] *n.* degree *(of temperature)*

хэн [khen] *pron.* who

хэн ч биш [khen ch bish] *pron.* nobody

хэрхэн [kher-khen] *adv.* how

хэрэв [khe-rev] *conj.* if

хэрэг [khe-reg] *n.* business

хэрэггүй [khe-reg-güi] *adj.* unnecessary

хэрэглэх [khe-reg-lekh] *v.* to use

хэрэгтэй [khe-reg-tei] *adj.* necessary, useful

хэрэгтэй байх [khe-reg-tei baikh] *v.* to need

хэсэг [khe-seg] *n.* section

хэцүү [khe-tsÜH] *adj.* difficult

хээр [khehr] *n.* valley

хялбар [khyal-bar] *adj.* easy, simple

хямд [khyamd] *adj.* cheap

хямдрал [khyamd-ral] *n.* 1. sale 2. discount

Ц

цаа буга [tsah bu-ga] *n.* reindeer

цаана [tsAH-na] *adv.* behind

цаас [tsahs] *n.* paper

цаашаа [tsAH-shAH] *adv.* keep away

цавуу [tsa-vUH] *n.* glue

цаг [tsag] *n.* 1. watch, clock *(time piece)* 2. hour
цаг агаар [tsag a-gAHr] *n.* weather
цагийн хувиар [tsa-gEEn khu-viar] *n.* schedule
цагаан [tsa-gAHn] *adj.* white
цагаан будаа [tsa-gAHn bu-dAH] *n.* *(white)* rice
цагаан хоолтон [tsa-gAHn khOHl-ton] *n.* vegetarian
цагаач [tsa-gAHch] *n.* immigrant
цагаачлах [tsa-gAHch-lakh] *v.* to immigrate
цагдаа [tsag-dAH] *n.* police *(man)*
цагдаагийн газар [tsag-dAH-gEEn ga-zar] *n.* police
     (station)
цадах [tsa-dakh] *v.* to be full
цай [tsai] *n.* tea
цайвар [tsai-var] *adj.* light *(in color)*
цайллага [tsail-la-ga] *n.* tea party
цалин [tsa-lin] *n.* salary, wages
цамц [tsamts] *n.* shirt
цангах [tsan-gakh] *v.* to be thirsty
царайлаг [tsa-rai-lag] *adj.* good-looking
цас [tsas] *n.* snow
цатгалан [tsat-ga-lan] *adj.* full
цахилгаан [tsa-khil-gAHn] *n.* electricity
цахилгаан [tsa-khil-gAHn] *n.* zipper
цахилгаан шат [tsa-khil-gAHn shat] *n.* elevator
цомог [tso-mog] *n.* album
цонх [tsonkh] *n.* window
цоож [tsohj] *n.* lock
цөөн [tsöhn] *adj.* few
цөцгий [tsöst-gEE] *n.* sour cream
цус [tsus] *n.* blood
цүнх [tsünkh] *n.* bag
цэвэр [tse-ver] *adj.* clean
цэвэрлэх [tse-ver-lekh] *v.* to clean
цэг [tseg] *n.* dot, point, period
цэглэх [tseg-lekh] *v.* to finish
цэнгэх [tsen-gekh] *v.* to have fun
цэс [tses] *n.* menu
цэцэг [tse-tseg] *n.* flower
цэцэрлэг [tse-tser-leg] *n.* 1. garden, park 2. kindergarten
цээж [tsehj] *n.* chest *(part of body)*
цээжлэх [tsEHj-lekh] *v.* to memorize

Ч

чагнах [chag-nakh] *v.* to hear
чадалтай [cha-dal-tai] *adj.* strong *(person)*
чадах [cha-dakh] *v.* to be able
чадвар [chad-var] *n.* ability
чамайг [cha-maig] *pron.* your
чанар [cha-nar] *n.* quality
чанах [cha-nakh] *v.* to cook
чанга [chan-ga] *adj.* loud
чармайх [char-maikh] *v.* to attempt, try
чек [chek] *n.* check *(bank)*
чи [chi] *pron.* you *(familiar form)*
чиг [chig] *n.* direction
чийдэн [chEE-den] *n.* light bulb
чиний [chi-nEE] *adj.* your
чинийх [chi-nEEkh] *pron.* yours
чих [chikh] *n.* ear
чихэвч [chi-khevch] *n.* headphones
чихэр [chi-kher] *n.* candy
чихэрлэг [chi-kher-leg] *adj.* sweet
чөлөөт [chö-lÖHt] *adj.* free *(not occupied with)*
чулуу [chu-lUH] *n.* rock, stone
чухал [chu-khal] *adj.* important
чүдэнз [chü-denz] *n.* matches

Ш

шаардах [shAHr-dakh] *v.* to demand
шагай [sha-gai] *n.* ankle
шавьж [shavij] *n.* bug, insect
шагнал [shag-nal] *n.* award
шалгалт [shal-galt] *n.* examination
шалгах [shal-gakh] *v.* to control, examine
шалтгаан [shalt-gAHn] *n.* reason
шар [shar] *adj.* yellow
шарах [sha-rakh] *v.* to fry
шат [shat] *n.* ladder, stairs
шатар [sha-tar] *n.* chess

шатах [sha-takh] *v.* to burn
шашин [sha-shin] *n.* religion
шиг [shig] *adj.* similar, like
шийгуа [shEE-gua] *n.* watermelon
шийдвэр [shEEd-ver] *n.* decision
шийдэх [shEE-dekh] *v.* to decide
шингэн [shin-gen] *n.* liquid
шинэ [shi-ne] *adj.* new
ширхэг [shir-kheg] *n.* single unit of, quantity of
ширээ [shi-rEH] *n.* table, desk
шоколад [sho-ka-lad] *n.* chocolate
шорон [sho-ron] *n.* jail
шороо [sho-rOH] *n.* soil
шошго [shosh-go] *n.* label
шөл [shöl] *n.* soup
шөнө [shö-nö] *n.* night
шувуу [shu-vUH] *n.* bird
шугам [shu-gam] *n.* 1. line 2. ruler *(measuring device)*
шулганах [shul-ga-nakh] *v.* to babble
шулуун [shu-lUhn] *adj.* straight
шуудан [shUH-dan] *n.* 1. mail 2. post office
шүд [shüd] *n.* tooth
шүдний эмч [shüd-nEE emch] *n.* dentist
шүлэг [shü-leg] *n.* poem
шүршүүр [shür-shÜHr] *n.* shower
шүүгч [shühgch] *n.* judge
шүүгээ [shÜH-gEH] *n.* cupboard, dresser
шүүлэг [shÜH-leg] *n.* test
шүүс [shühs] *n.* juice
шүүх [shühkh] *v.* to judge

Э

эв [ev] *n.* concord, peace
эвдрэл [evd-rel] *n.* damage
эвдрэх [evd-rekh] *v.* to be broken
эвдэх [ev-dekh] *v.* to break
эвлэл [ev-lel] *n.* union, league
эгч [egch] *n.* sister *(older)*

эгшиг [eg-shig] *n.* melody
эдгээх [ed-gEHkh] *v.* to cure
эдийн засаг [e-dEEn za-sag] *n.* economy
ээлдэг [e-yel-deg] *adj.* kind
эзэн [e-zen] *n.* owner
элбэг [el-beg] *adj.* abundant, plentiful
элемент [e-le-mEHnt] *n.* element
элч [elch] *n.* messenger
элчин сайд [el-chin said] *n.* ambassador
элчин сайдын яам [el-chin sai-dyn yAHm] *n.* embassy
эм [em] *n.* medicine, drug
эмийн жор [e-mEEn jor] *n.* prescription
эмнэлэг [em-ne-leg] *n.* hospital
эмч [emch] *n.* doctor
эмчлэх [emch-lekh] *v.* to treat
эмчилгээ [em-chil-gEH] *n.* treatment
эмэгтэй [e-meg-tei] *n.* woman
эмэгтэйчүүд [e-meg-tei-chÜHd] *n. pl.* women
эмэгчин [e-meg-chin] *adj.* female *(animal)*
эмээ [e-mEH] *n.* grandmother
эмээл [e-mEHl] *n.* saddle
энх тайван [enkh tai-van] *n.* peace
энэ [e-ne] *adj.* this
эр [er] *n.* male
эр хүн [er khün] *n.* man
эрвээхэй [er-vEH-khei] *n.* butterfly
эргэж ирэх [er-gej i-rekh] *v.* to go back, return
эргэлзэх [er-gel-zekh] *v.* to doubt, hesitate
эрдэм [er-dem] *n.* knowledge
эрдэмтэн [er-dem-ten] *n.* scientist
эрдэнэ [er-de-ne] *n.* treasure
эрин [e-rin] *n.* era
эрт [ert] *adj.* early
эртний [ert-nEE] *adj.* ancient, antique
эрүүл [e-rÜHl] *adj.* healthy
эрүүл мэнд [e-rÜHl mend] *n.* health
эрх [erkh] 1. *n.* right *(prerogative)* 2. *adj.* spoiled *(child)*
эрхлэгч [erkh-legch] *n.* director
эрхтэн [erkh-ten] *n.* organ *(human)*
эрхэм [er-khem] *adj., n.* dear

эрхүн [er-khün] *n.* gentleman
эрэгтэй [e-reg-tei] *n.* man
эрэл [e-rel] *n.* research
эрэх [e-rekh] *v.* to look for
эсгий [es-gEE] *n.* felt *(material)*
эсэргүүцэл [e-ser-gÜH-tsel] *n.* resistance
эсрэг [es-reg] *prep.* against
эх [ekh] *n.* 1. mother 2. source
эх орон [ekh o-ron] *n.* motherland
эхлэх [ekh-lekh] *v.* to begin
эхнэр [ekh-ner] *n.* wife
эцэг [e-tseg] *n.* father
эцэс төгсгөл [e-tses tögs-göl] *n.* end, ending
ээж [ehj] *n.* mom, mama
ээлж [ehlj] *n.* turn
ээмэг [EH-meg] *n.* earring

Ю

юм [yum] *n.* thing, stuff
юу [yUH] *adv.* what
юу [yÜH] *adv.* what
юутай [yu-tai] *adv.* with what

Я

ягаав [yAH-gAHv] *adv.* what happened
ягаад [yAH-gAHd] *adv.* why
ям [yahm] *n.* ministry
ямай [yAH-mai] *interj.* okay
яаралтай [yAH-ral-tai] *adv.* immediately
яарах [yAH-rakh] *v.* to hurry, to rush
яаруу [yAH-rUH] *adj.* hurried, rushed
ях вэ [yAHkh ve] *coll.* what is to be done?
явах [ya-vakh] *v.* to go
явган [yav-gan] *adv.* on foot
явган зорчигч [yav-gan zor-chigch] *n.* pedestrian
явдал [yav-dal] *n.* act; action

явуулах [ya-vUH-lakh] *v.* to send
явц [yavts] *n.* process
явцад [yav-tsad] *prep.* during
яг [yag] *adv.* exactly
ягаан [ya-gAHn] *adj.* pink
ядрах [yad-rakh] *v.* to be tired
ядуу [ya-dUH] *adj.* poor *(not rich)*
ял [yal] *n.* penalty, punishment
ялаа [ya-lAH] *n.* fly *(insect)*
ялагдах [ya-lag-dakh] *v.* to lose
ялах [ya-lakh] *v.* to win
ялгаа [yal-gAH] *n.* difference
ямаа [ya-mAH] *n.* goat
ямар [ya-mar] *adv.* which, what
ямх [yamkh] *n.* inch
янаг [ya-nag] *n.* sweetheart
янжуур [yan-jUHr] *n.* cigarette
ярилцлага [ya-rilts-la-ga] *n.* conversation
ярих [ya-rikh] *v.* to talk
яс [yas] *n.* bone
яттах [yat-gakh] *v.* to persuade

ENGLISH-MONGOLIAN DICTIONARY

A

a *art.* There is no indefinite article in Mongolian. Instead, НЭГ [neg] *should be used.*

abandon *v.* чөлөөтэй байх [chö-lÖH-tei baikh]

abbreviation *n.* товчилсон үг [tov-chil-son üg]

a.m *n.* ҮДЭЭС ӨМНӨ [ü-dEhs öm-nö]

ABC *n.* 1. цагаан толгой [tsa-gAHn tol-goi] *(alphabet)* 2. үндэс [ün-des] *(the basics)*

ability *n.* авъяас [av-YAHs], чадвар [chad-var]

about *prep.* 1. тухай [tu-khai] 2. орчим [or-chim] *(approximately)*

abroad *adv.* гадаадад [ga-dAH-dad]

absolutely *adv.* үнэхээр [ü-ne-khEHr]

abuse *v.* хүчирхийлэх [khü-chir-khEE-lekh]

accelerate *v.* хурдлах [khurd-lakh]

accent *n.* 1. аялга [a-yal-ga] 2. үгийн өргөлт [ü-gEEn ör-gölt]

accept *v.* хүлээн зөвшөөрөх [khü-lEHn zöv-shÖH-rökh]

accident *n.* аваар [a-vAHr]

accidental *adj.* санамсаргүй [sa-nam-sar-güi]

acclimatization *n.* идээшин суурьшилт [i-dEH-shin sUHri-shilt]

according to *prep.* ёсоор [yo-sOHr], дагуу [da-gUH]

account *n.* тооцоо [tOH-tsOH]

accountant *n.* нягтлан бодогч [nyagt-lan bo-dogch]

achievement *n.* ололт [o-lolt]

acknowledge *v.* хүлээн зөвшөөрөх [khü-lEHn zöv-shÖH-rökh]

acquaintance *n.* таних [ta-nil]

across *prep.* хөндлөн [khönd-lön]

action *n.* үйл хэрэг [üil khe-reg]

activate *v.* идэвхижүүлэх [i-dev-khi-jÜH-lekh]

activity *n.* идэвхи [i-dev-khi]

actor *n.* ЖҮЖИГЧИН [jü-jig-chin]

actually *adv.* ҮНЭНДЭЭ [ü-nen-dEH]

ad *n.* зар [zar], зарлал [zar-lal]

adapt *v.* нутагших [nu-tag-shikh]

add *v.* НЭМЭХ [ne-mekh]

addiction *n.* муу зуршил [muh zur-shil]

addition *n.* НЭМЭХ ҮЙЛДЭЛ [ne-mekh üil-del]

additional *adj.* НЭМЭЛТ [ne-melt]

address *n.* хаяг [kha-yag]

admit *v.* ҮНЭНЭЭ ХҮЛЭЭХ [ü-ne-nEH khü-lEHkh]

adopt *v.* ҮРЧЛЭХ [ürch-lekh]

adore *v.* ДЭЭДЛЭН ХҮНДЛЭХ [dEHd-len khühnd-lekh]

adult *n.* НАСАНД ХҮРЭГЧ [na-sand khü-regch]

advance *v.* 1. урагшлах [u-ragsh-lakh] *(proceed)*
        2. урьдчилах [urid-chi-lakh]

advantage *n.* завшаан [zav-shAHn], давуу тал
    [da-vUH tal]

adventure *n.* адал явдал [a-dal yav-dal]

advertisement *n.* зар [zar], зарлал [zar-lal]

advice *n.* ЗӨВӨЛГӨӨ [zö-völ-gÖH]

advise *v.* ЗӨВЛӨХ [zöv-lökh]

adviser *n.* ЗӨВЛӨГЧ [zöv-lögch]

after *adv.* ДАРАА [da-rAH], СҮҮЛД [sühld]

afternoon *n.* ҮДИЙН ХОЙНО [ü-dEEn khoi-no]

again *adv.* ДАХИН [da-khin]

against *prep.* ЭСРЭГ [es-reg]

age *n.* НАС [nas]

agency *n.* ТОВЧОО [tov-chOH]

ago *adv.* ӨМНӨ [öm-nö]

agreement *n.* ТОХИРОЛЦОЛ [to-khi-rol-tsol]

ahead *adv.* урагшаа [u-rag-shAH]

air *n.* агаар [a-gAHr], хий [khee]

air conditioner *n.* агааржуулагч
    [a-gAHr-jUH-lagch]

airplane *n.* ОНГОЦ [on-gots]

airport *n.* ОНГОЦны буудал [on-gots-ny bUH-dal]

alarm clock *n.* СЭРҮҮЛЭГ [se-rÜH-leg]

alcohol *n.* СОГТУУРУУЛАХ УНДАА [sog-tUH-rUH-lakh
    un-dAH]

alive *adj.* амьд [amid]

all *adj., n.* бүгд [bügd]
all right *adj.* зөв [zöv]
all together *adv.* бүгд [bügd]
almost *adv.* бараг [ba-rag]
alone *adj.* ганцаар [gan-tsAHr]
already *adv.* хэдийнэ [khe-dEE-ne]
also *adv.* түүнчлэн [tÜHn-chlen]
although *conj.*боловч [bo-lovch]
altitude *n.* өндөр газар [ön-dör ga-zar]
always *adv.* дандаа [dan-dAH], үргэлж [ür-gelj]
amazing *adj.* гайхалтай [gai-khal-tai]
ambassador *n.* элчин сайд [el-chin said]
ambulance *n.* түргэн тусламж [tür-gen tus-lamj]
among *prep.* хоорοнд [khOH-rond]
an *art.* See "a".
ancient *adj.* эртний [ert-nEE]
and *conj.* ба [ba]
angry *adj.* уурτай [UHr-tai]
animal *n.* амьтан [ami-tan], мал [mal] *(domesticated)*
ankle *n.* шагай [sha-gai]
anniversary *n.* ойн баяр [oin bayar]
announce *v.* зарлах [zar-lakh]
annoy *v.* уурлуулах [UHr-lUH-lakh]
annually *adv.* жил тутам [jil tu-tam]
another *adj.* өөр [öhr], бас нэг [bas neg]
answer *n.* хариу [kha-riu]
ant *n.* шоргоолж [shor-gOHlj]
antique *n.* хуучин эдлэл [khUH-chin ed-lel]
any *pron., adj.* аливаа [a-li-vAH]
anybody *pron.* хэн нэгэн [khen ne-gen]
anything *pron.* ямар нэгэн [ya-mar negen]
apart *adv.* тусдаа [tus-dAH]
apartment *n.* орон сууц [o-ron sUHts], байр [bair]
apologize *v.* уучлалт гуйх [UHch-lalt guikh]
apology *n.* уучлалт [UHch-lalt]
appendix *n.* 1. хавсралт [khavs-ralt] *(book)* 2. олгой
     [ol-goi] *(bodily organ)*
apple *n.* алим [a-lim]
application *n.* өргөдөл [ö-rög-döl]
appointment *n.* цаг товлоо [tsag tov-lOH]

appreciate *v.* талархах [ta-lar-khakh]
appreciation *n.* талархал [ta-lar-khal]
approximate *adj.* барагцаа [ba-rag-tsAH]
area *n.* орон зай [o-ron zai]
argue *v.* маргах [mar-gakh]
argument *n.* маргаан [mar-gAHn]
arm *n.* гар [gar]
around *adv.* эргэн тойрон [er-gen toi-ron]
arrange *v.* эмхлэх [emkh-lekh], цэгцлэх [tsegts-lekh]
arrive *v.* хүрч ирэх [khürch i-rekh]
art *n.* уран бүтээл [u-ran bü-tEHl]
artist *n.* зураач [zu-rAHch], жүжигчин [jü-jig-chin]
as soon as *conj.* аль болох хурдан [ali bo-lokh khur-dan]
as well as *conj.* аль болох сайн [ali bo-lokh sain]
ash *n.* үнс [üns]
ashtray *n.* үнсний сав [üns-nEE sav]
ask *v.* асуух [a-sUHkh]
ask for *v.* гуйх [guikh]
assignment *n.* даалгавар [dAHl-ga-var]
assist *v.* туслах [tus-lakh]
assistant *n.* зөвлөгч [zöv-lögch]
at home *adv.* гэртээ [ger-tEH]
at least *adv.* ядаж [ya-daj]
at once *adv.* ганц удаа [gants u-dah]
attempt *n.* чармайлт [char-mailt]; *v.* хичээх [khi-chEHkh]
attend *v.* оролцох [o-rol-tsokh]
attention *n.* анхаарал [an-khAH-ral]
attorney *n.* өмгөөлөгч [öm-gÖH-lögch]
aunt *n.* нагац [na-gats]
automatic *adj.* автомат [av-to-mat]
autumn *n.* намар [na-mar]
available *adj.* бололцоотой [bo-lol-tsOH-toi]
avenue *n.* өргөн чөлөө [ör-gön chö-lÖH]
average *adj.* дундаж [dun-daj]
avoid *v.* зайлсхийх [zails-khEEkh]
awake *v.* сэрэх [se-rekh], сэргэх [ser-gekh]
award *n.* шагнал [shag-nal]
awful *adj.* муухай [mUH-khai]
axe *n.* сүх [sükh]

B

babble *v.* шулганах [shul-ga-nakh]
baby *n.* нялх хүүхэд [nyalkh khÜH-khed]
bacon *n.* утсан гахайн мах [ut-san ga-khain makh]
bad *adj.* муу [muh]
bag *n.* цүнх [tsünkh]
baggage *n.* ачаа [a-chAH], тээш [tehsh]
bakery *n.* талхны мухлаг [talkh-ny mukh-lag]
ball *n.* бөмбөг [böm-bög]
banana *n.* банан [ba-nahn]
bank *n.* банк [bank]
bar *n.* бар [bahr]
barber *n.* үсчин [üs-chin]
bargain *n.* хямд [khyamd]
basis *n.* үндэс [ün-des], суурь [sUHri]
basket *n.* сагс [sags]
bathroom *n.* угаалгын өрөө [u-gAHl-gyn ö-rÖH],
    жорлон [jor-lon]
bathtub *n.* ванн [vann]
battery *n.* зай [zai]
be *v.* байх [baikh]
be afraid *v.* айх [aikh]
be hungry *v.* өлсөх [öl-sökh]
be right *v.* зөв байх [zöv baikh]
be sorry *v.* гэмших [gem-shikh]
be thirsty *v.* цангах [tsan-gakh]
be wrong *v.* буруу [bu-rUH]
beach *n.* далайн хөвөө [da-lain khö-vÖH]
bean *n.* буурцаг [bUHr-tsag]
bear *n.* баавгай [bAHv-gai]
beard *n.* сахал [sa-khal]
beautiful *adj.* сайхан [sai-khan], гоё [goyo]
beauty salon *n.* гоо сайхан [goh sai-khan]
because *conj.* учир [u-chir], тул [tul], яагаад гэвэл
    [yAH-gAHd ge-vel]
become *v.* болох [bo-lokh]
bed *n.* ор [or]
bed bug *n.* бясаа [bya-sAH]
bedroom *n.* унтлагын өрөө [unt-la-gyn ö-rÖH]

beef *n.* үхрийн мах [ükh-rEEn makh]
beefsteak *n.* бифштекс [bif-shteks]
beer *n.* пиво [pEE-vo]
beet *n.* манжин [man-jin]
before *prep.* өмнө [öm-nö]
begin *v.* эхлэх [ekh-lekh]
behind *adv.* хойно [khoi-no], ард [ard]
believe *v.* итгэх [it-gekh]
bell *n.* хонх [khonkh]
belong *v.* харъяалагдах [khar-yAH-lag-dakh]
below *adv.* доор [dohr], доош [dohsh]
belt *n.* бүс [büs], тэлээ [te-lEH]
besides *adv.* гадна [gad-na]
best *adj.* хамгийн сайн [kham-gEEn sain]
better *adv.* илүү сайн [i-lÜH sain], дээр [dehr]
between *prep.* хооронд [khOH-rond], дунд [dund]
beverage *n.* ундаа [un-dAH]
bicycle *n.* дугуй [du-gui]
big *adj.* том [tom]
bill *n.* тооцооны хуудас [tOH-tsOH-ny khUH-das]
bird *n.* шувуу [shu-vUH]
birth *n.* төрөлт [tö-rölt]
birthday *n.* төрсөн өдөр [tör-sön ö-dör]
black *adj.* хар [khar]
blackboard *n.* самбар [sam-bar]
blanket *n.* хөнжил [khön-jil]
blind *adj.* сохор [so-khor]
block *n.* хороолол [kho-rOH-lol]
blond *adj.* цайвар үст [tsai-var ust]
blood *n.* цус [tsus]
blue *adj.* хөх [khökh] *(dark)*, цэнхэр [tsen-kher] *(light)*
boat *n.* завь [zavi]
body *n.* бие [biye]
boil *v.* буцалгах [bu-tsal-gakh], чанах [cha-nakh]
book *n.* ном [nom]
bookstore *n.* номын дэлгүүр [no-myn del-gÜHr]
border *n.* хил [khil]
borrow *v.* зээлэх [zEH-lekh]
bottle *n.* лонх [lonkh]
bottom *n.* ёроол [yo-rOHl]

bowl *n.* аяга [a-ya-ga]

box *n.* хайрцаг [khair-tsag]

boy *n.* хүү [khüh]

boyfriend *n.* найз бандь [naiz bandi]

bracelet *n.* бугуйвч [bu-guivch]

brain *n.* тархи [tar-khi]

branch *n.* салбар [sal-bar], мөчир [mö-chir]

brand new *adj.* цоо шинэ [tsOH shi-ne]

bread *n.* талх [talkh]

break 1. *n.* завсарлага [zav-sar-la-ga] *(respite)*
    2. *v.* эвдэх [ev-dekh]

breakfast *n.* өглөөний цай [ög-lÖH-nEE tsai]

bribe *n.* хахууль [kha-khUHli]

bridge *n.* гүүр [gühr]

brief *adj.* товч [tovch]

bring *v.* авчрах [avch-rakh]

broad *adj.* өргөн [ör-gön]

broadcast *n.* нэвтрүүлэг [nevt-rÜH-leg]

broken *adj.* эвдэрсэн [ev-der-sen]

brother *n.* ах [akh] *(older)*, дүү (düh) *(younger)*

brown *adj.* хүрэн [khü-ren]

buddy *n.* найз [naiz]

budget *n.* төсөв [tö-söv]

bug *n.* шавьж [shavij]

building *n.* байшин [bai-shin]

bulb *n.* чийдэн [chEE-den] *(light)*

burn *v.* шатах [tsa-takh]

bus *n.* автобус [avto-buhs]

bus stop *n.* автобусны буудал [av-to-buhs-ny
    bUH-dal]

business *n.* ажил хэрэг [a-jil khe-reg]

business card *n.* нэрийн хуудас [ne-rEEn
    khUH-das]

but *conj.* гэвч [gevch]

butter *n.* тос [tos], масло [mahs-lo]

butterfly *n.* эрвээхэй [er-vEH-khei]

button *n.* товч [tovch]

buy *v.* худалдан авах [khu-dal-dan a-vakh]

buyer *n.* худалдан авагч [khu-dal-dan a-vagch]

by *prep.* -аар, -ээр, -оор, -уур [-ahr, -her, -ohr, -uhr]

C

cab *n.* такси [tak-si]
cabbage *n.* байцаа [bai-tsAH]
cable *n.* кабел [kah-bel]
café *n.* кафе [ka-feh]
cake *n.* торт [tohrt]
calendar *n.* календарь [ka-len-dari]
call *v.* 1. дуудах [dUH-dakh] 2. утасдах [u-tas-dakh]
    (by phone)
calm down *v.* тайтгарах [tait-ga-rakh]
camera *n.* зургийн аппарат [zur-gEEn ap-pa-raht]
camp *n.* зуслан [zus-lan]
can *n.* лааз [lahz]
candle *n.* лаа [lah]
candy *n.* чихэр [chi-kher]
canned food *n.* консерв [kon-sehrv]
canyon *n.* хавцал [khav-tsal]
capital *n.* нийслэл [nEEs-lel] *(city)*
car *n.* машин [ma-shin]
card *n.* 1. хөзөр [khö-zör] *(playing)* 2. карт [kahrt]
careful *adj.* болгоомжтой [bol-gOHmj-toi]
cargo *n.* онгоцны ачаа тээш [on-gots-ny a-chAH
    tehsh]
carpet *n.* хивс [khivs]
carrot *n.* лууван [lUH-van]
carry *v.* зөөх [zöhkh]
cart *n.* түрдэг тэрэг [tür-deg te-reg]
case *n.* хэрэг [khe-reg], явдал [yav-dal]
cash *n.* бэлэн мөнгө [be-len mön-gö]
cashier *n.* кассчин [kahss-chin]
cassette *n.* кассет [kas-syet]
cat *n.* муур [muhr]
catch up *v.* гүйцэх [gui-tsekh]
cathedral *n.* чогчин дуган [chog-chin du-gan]
cause *n.* шалтгаан [shalt-gAHn], учир [uchir]
caution *n.* сануулга [sa-nUHl-ga] *v.* анхааруулах
    [an-khAH-rUH-lakh]
cave *n.* агуй [agui]

ceiling *n.* тааз [tahz]

cellar *n.* зоорь [zOHri], подвал [pod-val]

cemetery *n.* оршуулгын газар [or-shUHl-gyn ga-zar]

central *adj.* төв [töv]

central heating *n.* төвлөрсөн халаалт [töv-lör-sön kha-lAHlt]

ceramics *n.* вааран эдлэл [vah-ran ed-lel]

ceremony *n.* ёслол [yos-lol]

certainly *adv.* тэгэлгүй яахав [te-gel-gui yAH-khav]

certificate *n.* гэрчилгээ [ger-chil-gEH]

chair *n.* сандал [san-dal]

chairman *n.* дарга [dar-ga]

challenge *n.* дуудлага [dUHd-la-ga]

champagne *n.* шампанск [sham-pahnsk]

champion *n.* аварга [a-var-ga]

change 1. *n.* өөрчлөлт [ÖHrch-lölt] 2. *v.* солих [so-likh]

charge *v.* төлөх [tö-lökh]

cheap *adj.* хямд [khaymd]

check 1. *n.* чек [chek] *(bank)* 2. *v.* шалгах [shal-gakh]

checkers *n.* даам [dAHm]

cheese *n.* бяслаг [byas-lag]

chemistry *n.* хими [khi-mi]

chess *n.* шатар [sha-tar]

chest *n.* цээж [tsehj] *(part of body)*

chewing gum *n.* бохь [bokhi]

chicken *n.* тахиа [ta-khia]

child *n.* хүүхэд [khÜH-khed]

chocolate *n.* шоколад [sho-ka-lahd]

choose *v.* сонгох [son-gokh]

Christmas *n.* зул сарын баяр [zul sa-ryn bayar]

church *n.* сүм [süm]

cigar *n.* навчин тамхи [nav-chin tam-khi]

cigarette *n.* янжуур [yan-jUHr]

cigarette lighter *n.* асаагуур [a-sAH-gUHr]

circle *n.* тойрог [toi-rog]

citizen *n.* иргэн [ir-gen]

city *n.* хот [khot]

class *n.* анги [angi] *(in school)*

classic *adj.* СОНГОДОГ [son-go-dog]
clean 1. *adj.* ЦЭВЭР [tse-ver] 2. *v.* ЦЭВЭРЛЭХ [tse-ver-lekh]
clerk *n.* ҮЙЛЧЛЭГЧ [üilch-legch]
climate *n.* УУР АМЬСГАЛ [uhr amis-gal]
climb *v.* АВИРАХ [avi-rakh]
clock *n.* ЦАГ [tsag]
close *adj.* 1. ОЙРХОН [oir-khon] 2. ДОТНО [dot-no] (*friend*)
close *v.* ХААХ [khahkh]
cloth *n.* НООСОН ДААВУУ [nOH-son dAH-vUH]
clothes *n.* ХУВЦАС [khuv-tsas]
clothes-hanger *n.* ӨЛГҮҮР [öl-gÜHr]
club *n.* КЛУБ [klub]
coal *n.* НҮҮРС [nührs]
coat *n.* ПАЛЬТО [pali-toh]
coffee *n.* КОФЕ [koh-fe]
cognac *n.* КОНЬЯК [kon-yak]
coin *n.* ЗООС [zohs]
cold *n.*, *adj.* ХҮЙТЭН [khüi-ten]
college *n.* КОЛЛЕЖ [kol-lehj]
color *n.* ӨНГӨ [ön-gö]
comb *n.* САМ [sam]
come *v.* ИРЭХ [i-rekh]
come down *v.* ТАЙТГАРАХ [tait-ga-rakh]
come in *v.* ОРЖ ИРЭХ [orj i-rekh]
Come in! *coll.* ОРООД ИР! [o-rOHd ir]
come out *v.* ГАДАА ГАРАХ [ga-dAH ga-rakh]
comfortable *adj.* ТУХТАЙ [tukh-tai]
comic *n.* ХОШИН [kho-shin]
commerce *n.* ХУДАЛДАА [khu-dal-dah]
commercial *adj.* ХУДАЛДААНЫ [khu-dal-dah-ny]
commission *n.* КОМИСС [ko-miss], ХОРОО [kho-rOH]
companion *n.* ТҮНШ [tünsh]
company *n.* КОМПАНИ [kom-pAH-ni]
compartment *n.* КУПЕ [ku-pEH] (*train*)
complain *v.* ГОМДОЛ ГАРАХ [gom-dol gar-gakh]
complete 1. *adj.* ТӨГС [tögs] 2. *v.* ГҮЙЦЭТГЭХ [güi-tset-gekh]
computer *n.* КОМПЬЮТЕР [kom-pyUH-ter]

concert *n.* концерт [kon-tsert]

conclusion *n.* дүгнэлт [düg-nelt]

condition *n.* нөхцөл [nökh-tsöl]

conference *n.* зөвлөлгөөн [zöv-löl-gÖHn]

congratulate *v.* баяр хүргэх [ba-yar khür-gekh]

Congratulations! *coll.* Баяр хүргэе! [ba-yar khür-ge-ye]

consider *v.* гэж үзэх [gej ü-zekh]

consign *v.* өгөх, тавих [ö-gökh, ta-vikh]

constant *adj.* тогтмол [togt-mol]

constitute *v.* бүрдүүлэх [bür-dÜH-lekh]

constitution *n.* үндсэн хууль [ünd-sen khUHli]

consulate *n.* консулын газар [kon-su-lyn ga-zar]

consult *v.* лавлах [lav-lakh], зөвлөх [zöv-lökh]

contact *n.* харилцаа [kha-ril-tsAH] *v.* холбоо барих [khol-boo ba-rikh]

contain *v.* агуулах [a-gUH-lakh]

container *n.* сав суулга [sav sUHl-ga]

content *adj.* утга санаа [ut-ga sa-nAH]

contents *n.* агуулга [a-gUHl-ga]

continent *n.* тив [tiv]

continuation *n.* үргэлжлэл [ür-gelj-lel]

continue *v.* үргэлжлүүлэх [ür-gelj-lÜH-lekh]

contract *n.* гэрээ [ge-rEH]

control *n.* хяналт [khya-nalt]

convenient *adj.* аятай [ay-tai], тохитой [to-khi-toi]

conversation *n.* яриллага [ya-rilts-la-ga]

converse *v.* ярих [ya-rikh], хөөрөх [khÖH-rökh]

cook 1. *n.* тогооч [to-gOHch] 2. *v.* чанах [cha-nakh]

cookie *n.* жигнэмэг [jig-ne-meg]

cool *adj.* сэрүүн [se-rÜHn]

copy *n.* 1. хувь [khuvi] 2. хуулбар [khUHl-bar]

corn *n.* тариа [ta-ria]

corner *n.* өнцөг [ön-tsög], булан [bu-lan]

corporation *n.* нэгдэл [neg-del]

corps *n.* корпус [kor-pus] *(e.g. peace corps)*

correct *adj.* зөв [zöv]

correspondent *n.* сурвалжлагч [sur-valj-lagch]

cost *n.* үнэ [ü-ne], өртөг [ör-tög]

cotton *n.* хөвөн [khö-vön]

count *v.* тоолох [tOH-lokh]

country *n.* улс [uls], орон [o-ron]
countryside *n.* хөдөө [khö-dOH]
cover 1. *n.* бүтээлэг [bu-tEH-leg] 2. хавтас
    [khav-tas] 3. *v.* бүтээх [bü-tEHkh]
cow *n.* үхэр [ü-kher]
crash *n.* сүйрэл [süi-rel]
crazy *adj.* галзуу [gal-zUH]
credit *n.* 1. ээл [zehl] 2. кредит [kre-dEEt]
crime *n.* гэмт хэрэг [gemt khe-reg]
cucumber *n.* өргөст хэмх [ör-göst khemkh]
culture *n.* соёл [so-yol]
cup *n.* аяга [a-ya-ga]
currency *n.* валют [va-lYUHt]
curtain *n.* хөшиг [khö-shig]
curve *n.* тахир [ta-khir], муруй [mu-rui]
custom *n.* ёс заншил [yos zan-shil] *(tradition)*
customer *n.* худалдан авагч [khu-dal-dan a-vagch]
customshouse *n.* гаалийн газар [gAH-lEEn ga-zar]
customs *n.* гааль [gAHli] *(on the border)*
cut *v.* зүсэх [zü-sekh]
cute *adj.* хөөрхөн [khÖHr-khön]

D

dad *n.* аав [ahv]
daily *adj.* өдөр тутмын [ö-dör tut-myn]
damage *n.* эвдрэл [evd-rel]
dance 1. *n.* бүжиг [bü-jig] 2. *v.* бүжиглэх [bü-jig-lekh]
danger *n.* аюул [a-yUHl]
dangerous *adj.* аюултай [a-yUHl-tai]
dark *adj.* харанхуй [kha-ran-khui]
darling *adj.* хонгор [khon-gor]
date *n.* 1. огноо [og-nOH] *(calendar)* 2. болзоо
    [bol-zOH] *(meeting)*
daughter *n.* охин [o-khin]
daughter-in-law *n.* бэр [ber]
day *n.* өдөр [ö-dör]
day after tomorrow *n.* нөгөөдөр [nö-gÖH-dör]
dear *adj.* эрхэм [er-khem]

death *n.* ҮХЭЛ [ü-khel]

debt *n.* ЗЭЭЛ [zehl]

decide *v.* ШИЙДЭХ [shEE-dekh]

decision *n.* ШИЙДВЭР [shEEd-ver]

declaration *n.* МЭДҮҮЛЭГ [me-dÜH-leg]

declare *v.* МЭДҮҮЛЭХ [me-dÜH-lekh]

deep *adj.* ГҮНЗГИЙ [günz-gEE]

degree *n.* 1. ХЭМ [khem] *(temperature)* 2. ЗЭРЭГ
[ze-reg] *(educational)*

delay *n.* ХОЙШ ТАВИХ [khoish ta-vikh]

delicious *adj.* АМТТАЙ [amt-tai]

deliver *v.* ХҮРГЭХ [khür-gekh]

demand *n.* ШААРДЛАГА [shAHrd-la-ga]

democracy *n.* АРДЧИЛАЛ [ard-chi-lal]

demonstrate *v.* ҮЗҮҮЛЭН ТАНИУЛАХ [üz-ÜHlen
ta-niu-lakh]

dentist *n.* ШҮДНИЙ ЭМЧ [shüd-nEE emch]

department *n.* ХЭЛТЭС [khel-tes]

department store *n.* ИХ ДЭЛГҮҮР [ikh del-gÜHr],
ТӨРӨЛ БҮРИЙН БАРААНЫ ДЭЛГҮҮР
[tö-röl bü-rEEn ba-rAh-ny del-gÜHr]

deposit *n.* УРЬДЧИЛГАА МӨНГӨ [urid-chil-gAH mön-gö]
(monetary)

describe *v.* ТОДОРХОЙЛОХ [to-dor-khoi-lokh]

desert *n.* ЦӨЛ [tsöl]

desire *n.* ТААЛАЛ [tah-lal]

dessert *n.* АМТТАН [amt-tan]

detail *n.* НАРИЙН ТОДОРХОЙ ХЭСЭГ [na-rEEn to-dor-khoi
khe-seg]

determine *v.* ТОДОРХОЙЛОХ [to-dor-khoi-lokh]

develop *v.* ХӨГЖҮҮЛЭХ [khög-jÜH-lekh]

diagnosis *n.* ОНОШ [o-nosh]

diamond *n.* АЛМААЗ [al-mAHz]

die *v.* ҮХЭХ [ü-khekh]

difference *n.* ЯЛГАА [yal-gAH]

difficult *adj.* АМАРГҮЙ [a-mar-güi], ХЭЦҮҮ [khe-tsÜH]

dinner *n.* ОРОЙН ХООЛ [o-roin khohl]

direct *adj.* ШУЛУУН [shu-lUHn]

direction *n.* ЗҮГ ЧИГ [züg chig]

director *n.* ЗАХИРАЛ [za-khi-ral]

dirt *n.* тоос [tohs], шороо [sho-rOH]

dirty *adj.* бохир [bo-khir]

discipline *n.* сахилга [sa-khil-ga]

discount *n.* хямдрал [khyamd-ral]

discover *v.* нээлт хийх [nehlt khEEkh]

discovery *n.* нээлт [nehlt]

discuss *v.* хэлэлцэх [khe-lel-tsekh]

dish *n.* сав суулга [sav sUHl-ga]

distance *n.* зай [zai]

distant *adj.* холын [kho-lyn]

distribute *v.* тараах [ta-rAHkh]

district *n.* район [ra-ion], дүүрэг [dÜH-reg]

disturb *v.* саад болох [sahd bo-lokh]

division *n.* хуваах үйлдэл [khu-vAHkh üil-del]

do *v.* хийх [kheekh]

doctor *n.* эмч [emch]

document *n.* баримт [ba-rimt], албан бичиг [al-ban
    bi-chig]

dog *n.* нохой [no-khoi]

door *n.* хаалга [khAHl-ga]

dot *n.* цэг [tseg]

double *adj.* давхар [dav-khar]

doubt *v.* эргэлзэх [er-gel-zekh]

dozen *n.* арван хоёр ширхэг [ar-van kho-yor
    shir-kheg]

drawer *n.* шүүгээний нүд [shÜH-gEH-nEE nüd]

dream *n.* 1. зүүд [zühd] *(when asleep)* 2. мөрөөдөл
    [mö-rÖH-döl] *(hope)*

dress *n.* даашинз [dAH-shinz]

dressed *(to get)* *v.* хувцаслах [khuv-tsas-lakh]

drink 1. *n.* ундаа [un-dAH] 2. *v.* уух [uhkh]

drive *v.* жолоодох [jo-lOH-dokh]

driver *n.* жолооч [jo-lOHch]

drop *v.* унагах [u-na-gakh]

drug *n.* эм [em]

drugstore *n.* эмийн сан [e-mEEn san]

drunk *adj.* согтуу [sog-tUH]

dry *adj.* хуурай [khUH-rai]

duck *n.* нугас [nu-gas]

during *prep.* явцад [yav-tsad], үед [ü-yed]

E

each *pron., adj.* бүхэн [bü-khen], бүр [bür]

ear *n.* чих [chikh]

early *adv.* эрт [ert]

earn *v.* хөдөлмөрлөх [khö-döl-mör-lökh]

earring *n.* ээмэг [EH-meg]

earthquake *n.* газар хөдлөл [ga-zar khöd-löl]

easily *adv.* хялбарханаар [khyal-bar-kha-nAHr]

east *n.* дорно [dor-no]

easy *adj.* амархан [a-mar-khan], хялбар [khyal-bar]

eat *v.* идэх [i-dekh]

economical *adj.* гамтai [gam-tai]

economy *n.* эдийн засаг [e-dEEn za-sag]

education *n.* боловсрол [bo-lovs-rol]

efficient *adj.* үр ашигтай [ür a-shig-tai]

egg *n.* өндөг [ön-dög]

eight *num.* найм [naim]

eighteen *num.* арван найм [ar-van naim]

eighty *num.* ная [naya]

election *n.* сонгууль [son-gUHli]

electricity *n.* цахилгаан [tsa-khil-gAHn]

elegant *adj.* ганган [gan-gan]

element *n.* элемент [e-le-mEHnt]

elephant *n.* заан [zAHn]

elevator *n.* цахилгаан шат [tsa-khil-gAHn shat]

eleven *num.* арван нэг [ar-van neg]

embassy *n.* элчин сайдын яам [el-chin sai-dyn yAHm]

emergency *n.* түргэн тусламж [tür-gen tus-lamj]

employ *v.* ажил олгох [a-jil ol-gokh]

employee *n.* ажилтан [a-jil-tan]

employment *n.* ажил эрхлэлт [a-jil erkh-lelt]

empty *adj.* хоосон [khOH-son]

end *n.* эцэс [e-tses], төгсгөл [tögs-göl]

engine *n.* мотор [mo-tor]

enough *adj., adv.* хангалттай [khan-galt-tai]

enter *v.* орж ирэх [orj i-rekh]

enterprise *n.* 1. самбаа [sam-bAH] 2. хэвшил [khev-shil]

entire *adj.* бүхэл [bü-khel], бүтэн [bü-ten]

entrance *n.* орох хаалга [o-rokh khAHl-ga]

envelope *n.* дугтуй [dug-tui]

environment *n.* байгаль орчин [bai-gali or-chin]

equal 1. *adj.* тэнцүү [ten-tsÜH] 2. *v.* тэнцэх [ten-tsekh]

equipment *n.* тоног төхөөрөмж [to-nog tö-khÖH-römj]

era *n.* эрин [e-rin]

erase *v.* арилгах [a-ril-gakh]

eraser *n.* баллуур [bal-lUHr]

especially *adv.* онцгой [onts-goi]

establish *v.* үндэслэх [ün-des-lekh]

estimate *n.* үнэлгээ [ü-nel-gEH]

eternal *adj.* үүрд [ührd]

even *adj.* тэгш [tegsh]

evening *n.* орой [o-roi], үдэш [ü-desh]

every *adj.* бүр [bür]

everybody *pron.* хүн бүр [khün bür]

everything *pron.* юм бүхэн [yum bü-khen]

everywhere *adv.* хаана ч [khAH-na ch]

exactly *adv.* яг [yag]

examination *n.* шалгалт [shal-galt]

examine *v.* шалгах [shal-gakh]

example *n.* жишээ [ji-shEH]; **for example** жишээ нь [ji-shEH ni];

excellent *adj.* гойд сайн [goid sain]

except *prep.* гадна [gad-na]

exchange *v.* солилцох [so-lil-tsokh]

excuse *n.* уучлалт [UHch-lalt]

excuse me *coll.* уучлана уу [UHch-la-na uh]

exercise *n.* дасгал [das-gal]

exhibition *n.* үзэсгэлэн [ü-zes-ge-len]

exit *n.* гарц [garts]

expect *v.* найдан хүлээх [nai-dan khü-lEHkh]

expense *n.* зарлага [zar-la-ga]

expensive *adj.* үнэтэй [ü-ne-tei]

explain *v.* тайлбарлах [tail-bar-lakh]

explanation *n.* тайлбар [tail-bar]

export 1. *n.* экспорт [eks-port] 2. *v.* экспортлох [eks-port-lokh]

exterior *n.* гадна тал [gad-na tal]

extra *adj.* ИЛҮҮ [i-lÜH]
extraordinary *adj.* ОНЦГОЙ [onts-goi]
extremely *adv.* ТУЙЛЫН [tui-lyn]
eye *n.* НҮД [nüd]
eyebrow *n.* ХӨМСӨГ [khöm-sög]
eyeglasses *n.* НҮДНИЙ ШИЛ [nüd-nEE shil]
eyelash *n.* СОРМУУС [sor-mUHs]

F

fabric *n.* БӨС ДААВУУ [bös dAH-vUH]
face *n.* НҮҮР [nühr]
factory *n.* ҮЙЛДВЭР [üild-ver]
fail *v.* НУРАХ [nu-rakh]
failure *n.* БҮТЭЛГҮЙТЭЛ [bü-tel-güi-tel]
fall *v.* ОЙЧИХ [oi-chikh], УНАХ [u-nakh]
false *adj.* ХУДАЛ [khu-dal]
familiar *adj.* ТАНИЛ [ta-nail]
family *n.* АЙЛ ГЭР [ail ger], ГЭР БҮЛ [ger bül]
famous *adj.* АЛДАРТАЙ [al-dar-tai]
fantastic *adj.* ЕР БУСЫН [yer bu-syn]
far *adv.* АЛС [als], ХОЛ [khol]
farm *n.* ФЕРМ [ferm]
fast *adj.* ХУРДАН [khur-dan]
fat 1. *n.* ӨӨХ [öhkh] 2. *adj.* ТАРГАН [tar-gan]
father *n.* ЭЦЭГ [e-tseg], ААВ [ahv]
father-in-law *n.* ХАДАМ ААВ [kha-dam ahv]
fear *n.* АЙДАС [ai-das]
fee *n.* ТӨЛБӨР [töl-bör]
feel *v.* МЭДРЭХ [med-rekh]
female *adj.* ЭМ [em], ЭМЭГЧИН [e-meg-chin] *(animal)*
fence *n.* ХАШАА [kha-shAH]
festival *n.* ФЕСТИВАЛЬ [fes-ti-vali]
fever *n.* ХАЛУУРАЛТ [kha-lUH-ralt]
few *adj.* ЦӨӨН [tsöhn]
fifteen *num.* АРВАН ТАВ [ar-van tav]
fifty *num.* ТАВЬ [tavi]
fight *n.* ЗОДООН [zo-dOHn]
file *n.* ХАВТАС [khav-tas]

film *n.* кино [ki-no]

finance *n.* хөрөнгө [khö-rön-gö], санхүү [san-khÜH]

find *v.* олох [o-lokh]

Fine! *coll.* Болно! [bol-no]

finger *n.* хуруу [khu-rUH]

finish *v.* дуусах [dUH-sakh]

fire *n.* гал түймэр [gal tüi-mer]

first *ord.* нэгдүгээр [neg-dü-gEHr]

fish *n.* загас [za-gas]

fishing *n.* загасчлах [za-gasch-lakh]

five *num.* тав [tav]

fix *v.* засах [za-sakh]

flag *n.* туг [tug]

flight *n.* нислэг [nis-leg]

flood *n.* үер [ü-yer]

floor *n.* 1. шал [shal] 2. давхар [dav-khar] *(story)*

flour *n.* гурил [gu-ril]

flower *n.* цэцэг [tse-tseg]

flu *n.* ханиад [kha-niad]

fly 1. *n.* ялаа [ya-lAH] 2. *v.* нисэх [ni-sekh]

fog *n.* манан [ma-nan]

folder *n.* хавтас [khav-tas]

follow *v.* дагах [da-gakh]

food *n.* хоол [khohl]

food market *n.* хүнсний зах [khüns-nEE zakh]

foot *n.* хөл [khöl]

football *(Amer.)* *n.* хөл бөмбөг [khöl böm-bög]

for *prep.* тул [tul], төлөө [tö-lÖH]

forehead *n.* дух [dukh]

foreign *adj.* гадаад [ga-dAHd]

forest *n.* ой [oi]

forget *v.* мартах [mar-takh]

fork *n.* сэрээ [se-rEH]

form *n.* 1. хэлбэр [khel-ber] *(shape)* 2. маягт [ma-yagt] *(application)*

fortunately *adv.* azaar [a-zAHr]

fortune 1. *n.* аз завшаан [az zav-shAHn] 2. хувь заяа [khuvi za-yAH] *(destiny)*

forty *num.* дөч [döch]

foundation *n.* фонд *[fond]*

four *num.* ДӨРӨВ [dö-röv]
fourteen *num.* арван дӨрӨв [ar-van dö-röv]
fourth *ord.* дӨрӨвдүгээр [dö-röv-dü-ger]
fox *n.* үнэг [ü-neg]
frame *n.* жааз [jAHz]
free *adj.* чӨлӨӨт [chö-lÖHt]
freedom *n.* эрх чӨлӨӨ [erkh chö-lÖH]
free time *n.* зав [zav], чӨлӨӨт цаг [chö-lÖHt tsag]
freeze *v.* хӨлдӨх [khöl-dökh]
frequently *adv.* олон тохиолдох [o-lon to-khiol-dokh]
fresh *adj.* шинэ [shi-ne]
Friday *n.* баасан [bAH-san]
friend *n.* найз [naiz]
friendly *adj.* найрсаг [nair-sag]
friendship *n.* найрамдал [nai-ram-dal]
frog *n.* мэлхий [mel-khEE]
from *prep.* ...аас, ...ээс [...aas, ...ees]
fruit *n.* жимс [jims]
fry *v.* шарах [sha-rakh]
full 1. *adj.* цатгалан [tsat-ga-lan] 2. *v. (to be)* цадах [tsa-dakh]
fun *n.* зугаа [zu-gAH]
funny *adj.* зугаатай [zu-gAH-tai]
furniture *n.* тавилга [ta-vil-ga]
future *n.* ирээдүй [i-rEH-düi]

G

gallon *n.* галлон [gal-lOHn]
game *n.* тоглоом [tog-lOHm], наадам [nAH-dam]
garage *n.* гараж [ga-raj]
garbage *n.* хог [khog]
garden *n.* цэцэрлэг [tse-tser-leg]
garlic *n.* сармис [sar-mis]
gas *n.* 1. хий [khee] 2. бензин [ben-zin] *(for motor vehicles)*
general *adj.* ерөнхий [yö-rön-khEE]
generous *adj.* өгөөмөр [ö-gÖH-mör]
genius *n.* сүүт [suht]

gentleman *n.* эрхүн [er-khün]
genuine *adj.* жинхэнэ [jin-khe-ne]
get *v.* авах [a-vakh]
get up *n.* босох [bo-sokh]
get used to *v.* дадах [da-dakh]
gift *n.* бэлэг [be-leg]
gin *n.* джин [jeen]
girl *n.* охин [o-khin]
give *v.* өгөх [ö-gökh]
glad *(to be)* *v.* баярлах [ba-yar-lakh]
glass *n.* шил [shil]
glasses *n.* нүдний шил [nüd-nEE shil]
gloves *n.* бээлий [bEH-lEE]
glue *n.* цавуу [tsa-vUH]; *v.* наах [nahkh]
go *v.* явах [ya-vakh]
go away *v.* зайлах [zai-lakh]
go back *v.* эргэж ирэх [er-gej i-rekh]
go home *v.* харих [kha-rinkh]
go out *v.* гадагш гарах [ga-dagsh ga-rakh]
go shopping *v.* худалдан авах [khu-dal-dan a-vakh]
goal *n.* зорилго [zoril-go]
goat *n.* ямаа [ya-mAH]
Gobi desert *n.* говь [govi]
god *n.* бурхан [bur-khan]
gold *n.* алт [alt]
good *adj.* сайн [sain]
good-bye *n.* баяртай [ba-yar-tai]
good-looking *adj.* царайлаг [tsa-rai-lag]
goods *n.* бараа [ba-rAH]
government *n.* засгийн газар [zas-gEEn ga-zar]
governor *n.* засаг дарга [za-sag dar-ga]
grammar *n.* хэлзүй [khel züi]
granddaughter *n.* ач охин [ach o-khin]
grandfather *n.* өвөө [ö-vÖH]
grandmother *n.* эмээ [e-mEH]
grandson *n.* ач хүү [ach khüh]
grape *n.* усан үзэм [u-san ü-zem]
grateful *(to be)* *v.* талархах [ta-lar-khakh]
gravy *n.* сүүмс [sühms]
gray *adj.* буурал [bUH-ral]

great *adj.* агуу [a-gUH]
green *adj.* ногоон [no-gohn]
greet *v.* мэндлэх [mend-lekh]
greeting *n.* мэндчилгээ [mend-chil-gEH]
grocery *n.* хүнсний зүйлс [khüns-nEE züils]
ground *n.* газар [ga-zar]
guarantee *n.* баталгаа [ba-tal-gAH]
guard 1. *n.* хамгаалалт [kham-gAH-lalt]
      2. *v.* хамгаалах [kham-gAH-lakh]
guess *n.* таамаг [tah-mag]
guest *n.* зочин [zo-chin]
guide *n.* газарч [ga-zarch]
guidebook *n.* лавлах толь [lav-lakh toli]
guilty *adj.* буруутай [bu-rUH-tai]
gum *n.* бохь [bokhi] *(chewing)*
gun *n.* буу [buh]

H

habit *n.* зуршил [zur-shil]
hair *n.* үс [üs]
hairdresser *n.* үсчин [üs-chin]
half *adj.* хагас [kha-gas]
hall *n.* танхим [tan-khim]
ham *n.* утсан хиам [ut-san khiam]
hand *n.* гар [gar]
handbag *n.* гар цүнх [gar tsünkh]
handle *n.* бариул [ba-riul]
handsome *adj.* царайлаг [tsa-rai-lag]
hanger *n.* өлгүүр [öl-gÜHr] *(for clothes)*
happen *v.* тохиолдох [to-khiol-dokh]
happiness *n.* аз жаргал [az jar-gal]
happy *adj.* азтai [az-tai]
hard *adj.* 1. хатуу [kha-tUH] *(not soft)* 2. хэцүү
      [khe-tsÜH] *(not easy)*
hat *n.* малгай [mal-gai]
hate *v.* үзэн ядах [ü-zen ya-dakh]
have *v.* авах [a-vakh]
have fun *v.* хөгжилдөх [khög-jil-dökh]

hay *n.* өвс [övs]

he *pron.* тэр (эрэгтэй) [ter (e-reg-tei)]

head *n.* толгой [tol-goi]

headache *n.* толгой өвдөх [tol-goi öv-dökh]

headphone *n.* чихэвч [chi-khevch]

health *n.* эрүүл мэнд [e-rÜHl mend]

healthy *adj.* эрүүл [e-rÜHl]

hear *v.* сонсох [son-sokh], чагнах [chag-nakh]

heart *n.* зүрх [zürkh]

heat *n.* халаалт [kha-lAHlt]

heavy *adj.* хүнд [khünd]

heel *n.* өсгий [ös-gEE]

height *n.* өндөр [ön-dör]

help *v.* туслах [tus-lakh]

Help! *coll.* Туслаач! [tus-lAHch], Туслаарай! [tus-lAH-rai]

herdsman *n.* малчин [mal-chin]

here *adv.* энд [end]

heritage *n.* өв [öv]

hesitate *v.* эргэлзэх [er-gel-zekh]

hey *interj.* хөөе [khöh-ye]

hide *v.* нуух [nuhkh]

highway *n.* хурдны зам [khurd-ny zam]

hire *v.* ажилд авах [a-jild a-vakh]

hole *n.* цоорхой [tsOHr-khoi]

holiday *n.* баяр [ba-yar]

home *n.* гэр [ger]

homeland *n.* нутаг [nu-tag]

honest *adj.* үнэнч [ü-nench]

honey *n.* бал [bal]

honeymoon *n.* бал сар [bal sar]

hope 1. *n.* найдвар [naid-var], итгэл [it-gel]
      2. *v.* найдах [nai-dakh]

horse *n.* адуу [a-dUH] (*generic term*), морь [mori]

hospital *n.* эмнэлэг [em-ne-leg]

hot *adj.* халуун [kha-lUHn]

hot-dog *n.* зайдастай талх [zai-das-tai talkh]

hotel *n.* зочид буудал [zo-chid bUH-dal]

hour *n.* цаг [tsag]

house *n.* байшин [bai-shin]

how *adv.* хэрхэн [kher-khen]
how many *adv.* хэд [khed], хэдэн [khe-den]
how much *adv.* хэдий чинээн [khe-dEE chi-nEEn]
hundred *num.* зуу [zuh]
hungry *(to be)* *v.* өлсөх [öl-sökh]
hunt *v.* ан хийх [an khEEkh]
hunter *n.* анчин [an-chin]
hurry *v.* яарах [yAH-rakh]
husband *n.* нөхөр [nö-khör]

I

I *pron.* би [bi]
ice *n.* мөс [mös]
ice cream *n.* мөхөөлдөс [mö-khÖHl-dös], зайрмаг
    [zair-mag]
idea *n.* санаа [sa-nAH]
identity card *n.* биеийн байцаалт [bi-ye-EEn
    bai-tsAHlt]
if *conj.* хэрэв [khe-rev]
ill *adj.* өвчтэй [övch-tei]
illegal *adj.* хууль бус [khUHli bus]
illness *n.* өвчин [öv-chin]
imagine *v.* дүрслэн бодох [dürs-len bo-dokh]
immediate *adj.* даруй [da-rui]
immigrant *n.* цагаач [tsa-gAHch]
immigrate *v.* цагаачлан ирэх [tsa-gAHch-lan i-rekh]
important *adj.* чухал [chu-khal]
impossible *adj.* боломжгүй [bo-lomj-güi]
impress *v.* сэтгэгдэл төрүүлэх [set-geg-del
    tö-rÜH-lekh]
impression *n.* сэтгэгдэл [set-geg-del]
improve *v.* сайжруулах [saij-rUH-lakh]
in *prep.* ... д, ...т [...d, ..t]; дотор [do-tor]
in advance *adv.* урьдчилан [urid-chi-lan]
inch *n.* инч [inch], ямх [yamkh]
include *v.* багтаах [bag-tAHkh]
including *prep.* оролцуулан [o-rol-tsUH-lan]
income *n.* орлого [or-lo-go]

income tax *n.* орлогын татвар [or-lo-gyn tat-var]
incorrect *adj.* буруу [bu-rUH]
increase *v.* өсгөх [ös-gökh]
independent *adj.* бие даасан [biye dAH-san], чөлөөт [chö-lÖHt]
industry *n.* аж үйлдвэр [aj üild-ver]
inexpensive *adj.* үнэтэй бус [ü-ne-tei bus]
initiative *n.* санаачлага [sa-nAHch-la-ga]
innocent *adj.* буруугүй [bu-rUH-güi]
insect *n.* хорхой [khor-khoi]
inside *adv.* дотор талд [do-tor tald]
inspect *v.* шалгалт хийх [shal-galt kheekh]
instead of *prep.* … ний оронд [… nee o-rond]
institute *n.* дээд сургууль [dEHd sur-gUHli]
instruction *n.* зааварчилга [zAH-var-chil-ga]
insult *v.* гомдоох [gom-dOHkh]
insurance *n.* даатгал [dAHt-gal]
insure *v.* даатгах [dAHt-gakh]
intellectual *n.* оюуны өмч [o-yUH-ny ömch]
intelligent *adj.* сэхээтэний [se-khEH-te-nEE]
interest *n.* сонирхол [so-nir-khol]
interesting *adj.* сонирхолтой [so-nir-khol-toi]
interpreter *n.* хэлмэрч [khel-merch]
intersection *n.* уулзвар [uhlz-var]
into *prep.* … дотор [do-tor]
introduce *v.* танилцуулах [ta-nil-tsUH-lakh]
invitation *n.* урилга [u-ril-ga]
invite *v.* урих [u-rikh]
iron *n.* 1. индүү [in-dÜH] *(appliance)* 2. төмөр [tö-mör] *(metal)*
island *n.* арал [a-ral]
item *n.* зүйл [züil], ширхэг [shir-kheg]

J

jacket *n.* хүрэм [khü-rem], куртка [kuhrt-ka]
jail *n.* шорон [sho-ron]
jewelry *n.* алт мөнгөн эдлэл [alt mön-gön ed-lel]
job *n.* ажил [a-jil]

joke *n.* наргиа [nar-gia]
judge *v., n.* ШҮҮХ [shühkh]
juice *n.* ШҮҮС [shühs]
jump *v.* харайх [kha-raikh]
just *adv.* дөнгөж сая [dön-göj saya]
justice *n.* ШҮҮХ [shühkh]

K

keep *v.* хадгалах [khad-ga-lakh]
keep away *adv.* цаашаа [tsAH-shAH]
key *n.* түлхүүр [tül-khÜHr]
kids *n.* багачууд [ba-ga-chUHd]
kill *v.* алах [a-lakh]
kilogram *n.* килограмм [ki-lo-grAHm]
kilometer *n.* километр [ki-lo-metr]
kind *adj.* эелдэг [e-yel-deg]
king *n.* хаан [khahn]
kiss *n.* үнсэх [ün-sekh]
kitchen *n.* галын өрөө [ga-lyn ö-rÖH]
knee *n.* өвдөг [öv-dög]
knife *n.* хутга [khut-ga]
knock *v.* тогших [tog-shikh]
know *v.* мэдэх [me-dekh]
knowledge *n.* мэдлэг [med-leg]

L

label *n.* шошго [shosh-go]
labor *n.* хөдөлмөр [khö-döl-mör]
lace *n.* 1. тор [tor] 2. үдээс [ü-dEHs] *(shoe)*
lack *n.* дутагдах [du-tag-dakh]
ladder *n.* шат [shat]
lady *n.* бүсгүй [büs-güi]
lake *n.* нуур [nuhr]
lama *n.* лам [lam]
lamp *n.* чийдэн [chEE-den]
land 1. *n.* газар [ga-zar] 2. *v.* газардах [ga-zar-dakh]

language *n.* ХЭЛ [khel]

large *adj.* ТОМ [tom]

last *adj.* СҮҮЛИЙН [sÜH-lEEn]

last name *n.* ОВОГ [ovog]

last year *n.* НӨДНИН [nod-ning]

late *adv.* ОРОЙТСОН [o-roit-son]

laugh 1. *n.* ИНЭЭД [i-nEHd] 2. *v.* ИНЭЭХ [i-nEHkh]

laundry *n.* угаалга [u-gAHl-ga]

law *n.* хууль [khUHli]

lawyer *n.* хуульч [khUHlich]

lazy *adj.* залхуу [zal-khUH]

leader *n.* удирдагч [u-dir-dagch]

leaf *n.* навч [navch]

learn *v.* судлах [sud-lakh]

least *adj.* ӨЧҮҮХЭН [ö-chÜH-khen]

leather *n.* савхи [sav-khi]

leave *v.* үлдээн одох [ül-dEHn o-dokh]

left *adj.* ЗҮҮН [zühn]

leg *n.* ХӨЛ [khöl]

legal *adj.* хууль ёсны [khUHli yos-ny]

lemon *n.* нимбэг [nim-beg]

lemonade *n.* нимбэгийн ундаа [nim-be-gEEn un-dAH]

length *n.* урт [urt]

less *adj., adv.* бага [ba-ga]; дутуу [du-tUH]

lesson *n.* хичээл [khi-chEHl]

letter *n.* 1. захиа [za-khia] 2. ҮСЭГ [ü-seg] *(of alphabet)*

library *n.* номын сан [no-myn san]

license *n.* ҮНЭМЛЭХ [ü-nem-lekh]

lie *n.* худал хэлэх [khu-dal khe-lekh]

life *n.* амьдрал [amid-ral]

light *n.* гэрэл [ge-rel]; *adj.* цайвар [tsai-var], ХӨНГӨН [khöl-rökh]

light bulb *n.* ЧИЙДЭН [chEE-den]

like *v.* дуртай байх [dur-tai baikh], таалагдах [tAH-lag-dakh]

liquid *n.* ШИНГЭН [shin-gen]

liquor *n.* ЛИКОР [li-kor]

list *n.* нэрсийн жагсаалт [ner-sEEn jag-sAHlt]

listen *v.* СОНСОХ [son-sokh]

literature *n.* ЗОХИОЛ [zo-khiol]

little *adj.* жижиг [ji-jig]
live *v.* амьдрах [amid-rakh]
lobster *n.* хавч [khavch]
location *n.* байршил [bair-shil]
lock *n.* цоож [tsohj]
long *adj.* урт [urt]
look at *v.* харах [kha-rakh]
look for *v.* эрэх [e-rekh]
look like *v.* адилхан байх [a-dil-khan baikh]
lose *v.* 1. гээх [gehkh] *(mislay)* 2. ялагдах [ya-lag-dakh]
        (fail to win)
lottery *n.* сугалаа [su-ga-lAH]
loud *adj.* чанга [chan-ga]
love 1. *n.* хайр [khair] 2. *v.* хайрлах [khair-lakh]
luck *n.* аз [az]
luggage *n.* ачаа [a-chAH]
lunch *n.* өдрийн хоол [öd-rEEn khohl]
luxury *n.* тансаг [tan-sag]

M

machine *n.* машин [ma-shin]
magazine *n.* сэтгүүл [set-gÜHl]
mail 1. *n.* шуудан [shUH-dan] 2. *v.* илгээх [il-gEHkh]
main *adj.* гол [gol], үндсэн [ünd-sen]
main square *n.* төв талбай [töv tal-bai]
make *v.* хийх [khEEkh], үйлдвэрлэх [üld-ber-lekh]
make a mistake *v.* алдаа гаргах [al-dAH gar-gakh]
make sure *v.* лавлах [lav-lakh]
male *n.* эр [er]
man *n.* эрэгтэй хүн [e-reg-tei khün]
manager *n.* эрхлэгч [erkh-legch]
many *adj.* олон [o-lon]
map *n.* газрын зураг [gaz-ryn zu-rag]
market *n.* зах [zakh]
marmot *n.* тарвага [tar-va-ga]
married *adj.* гэрлэсэн [ger-le-sen]
marry *v.* гэрлэх [ger-lekh]
mask *n.* баг [bag]

match *(athletic)* *n.* ТЭМЦЭЭН [tem-tsEHn]
matches *n.* ЧҮДЭНЗ [chü-denz]
me *pron.* би [bi], надад [na-dad]
meal *n.* ЗООГ [zOHg], ХООЛ [khohl]
meat *n.* мах [makh]
medicine *n.* эм [em]
meet *v.* уулзах [UHl-zakh]
meeting *n.* хурал [khu-ral]
melody *n.* ЭГШИГ [eg-shig]
melon *n.* гуа [guah]
memorize *v.* цээжлэх [tsEHj-lekh]
memory *n.* дурсгал [durs-gal]
menu *n.* ЦЭС [tses]
merchandise *n.* бараа [ba-rAH]
message *n.* МЭДЭЭЛЭЛ [me-dEH-lel]
messenger *n.* ЭЛЧ [elch]
meter *n.* ТООЛУУР [tOH-lUHr]
milk *n.* СҮҮ [süh]
million *num.* сая [saya]
mine *pron.* МИНИЙХ [mi-nEEkh]
minister *n.* САЙД [said]
ministry *n.* яам [yAHm]
minus *n.* хасах [kha-sakh]
minute *n.* минут [mi-nut]
mirror *n.* ТОЛЬ [toli]
Miss *n.* ГЭРЛЭЭГҮЙ ЭМЭГТЭЙ [ger-lEH-güi e-meg-tei]
miss *v.* 1. санах [sa-nakh] (feel the lack of) 2. таслах
 [tas-lakh] *(fail to attend)*
mistake *n.* алдаа [al-dAH]
mister *n.* гуай [guai]
modern *adj.* орчин үеийн [or-chin ü-ye-EEn]
moment *n.* агшин [ag-shin]
Monday *n.* даваа [da-vAH]
money *n.* мөнгө [mön-gö]
money order *n.* мөнгө гуйвуулах [mön-gö
 gui-vUH-lakh]
Mongolian 1. *n.* МОНГОЛ ХҮН [mong-gol khün] 2. *adj.*
 МОНГОЛЫН [mong-go-lyn]
monk *n.* лам [lam] *(Buddhist)*
monkey *n.* сармагчин [sar-mag-chin]

month *n.* сар [sar]
monument *n.* хөшөө [khö-shÖH]
moon *n.* сар [sar]
more *adv.* илүү их [i-lÜH ikh]
morning *n.* өглөө [ög-lÖH]
mosquito *n.* шумуул [shu-mUHl]
most *n.* хамгийн [kham-gEEn]
mother *n.* ээж [ehj], эх [ekh]
mother-in-law *n.* хадам ээж [kha-dam ehj]
motherland *n.* эх орон [ekh o-ron]
mountain *n.* уул [uhl]
mouth *n.* ам [am]
move *v.* нүүх [nühkh]
movement *n.* хөдөлгөөн [khö-döl-gÖHn]
movie *n.* кино [ki-no]
movie theater *n.* кино театр [ki-no te-atr]
much *adj., adv.* их [ikh]
multiplication *n.* үржих үйлдэл [ür-jikh üil-del]
museum *n.* музей [mu-zei]
mushroom *n.* мөөг [mÖHg]
music *n.* хөгжим [khög-jim]
musician *n.* хөгжимчин [khög-jim-chin]
must *aux.* ёстой [yos-toi]
my *adj.* миний [mi-nEE]
myself *pron.* би өөрөө [bi ÖH-rÖH]

N

name *n.* нэр [ner]
nap *n.* дуг хийх [dug khEEkh]
napkin *n.* амны алчуур [am-ny al-chUHr]
nation *n.* үндэстэн [ün-des-ten]
national *adj.* үндэсний [ün-des-nEE]
nationality *n.* үндэстэн [ün-des-ten]
nature *n.* байгаль [bai-gali] *(natural world)*
near *adv.* ойролцоо [oi-rol-tsOH]
necessary *adj.* хэрэгтэй [khe-reg-tei]
neck *n.* хүзүү [khü-zÜH]
need *v.* хэрэгтэй байх [khe-reg-tei baikh]

negative *adj.* сөрөг [sö-rög]
neighbor *n.* хөрш [khörsh]
network *n.* сүлжээ [sül-jEH]
never *adv.* хэзээ ч үгүй [khe-zEH ch ü-güi]
new *adj.* шинэ [shi-ne]
news *n.* мэдээ [me-dEH]
newspaper *n.* сонин [so-nin]
next *adj.* дараачийн [da-rAH-chEEn]
next year *n.* хойтон [khoi-ton]
nice *adj.* сайн [sain]
nickname *n.* хоч [khoch]
night *n.* шөнө [shö-nö]
nine *num.* ес [yös]
nineteen *num.* арван ес [ar-van yös]
ninety *num.* ер [yer]
ninth *ord.* есдүгээр [yös-dü-gEHr]
no *adj.* үгүй [ü-güi], биш [bish]
nobody *pron.* хэн ч биш [khen ch bish]
noise *n.* дуу чимээ [duh chi-mEH]
nomad *n.* нүүдэлчин [nÜH-del-chin]
noon *n.* үд [üd]
·**north** *n.* хойд [khoid]
nose *n.* хамар [kha-mar]
note *n.* тэмдэглэл [tem-deg-lel]
nothing *pron.* юу ч биш [yUH ch bish]
now *adv.* одоо [o-dOH]
number *n.* тоо [toh]
nurse *n.* сувилагч [su-vi-lagch]

O

observe *v.* ажиглах [a-jig-lakh]
obtain *v.* олж авах [olj a-vakh]
occupation *n.* мэргэжил [mer-ge-jil]
occupy *v.* эзлэх [ez-lekh]
occur *v.* болох [bo-lokh]
of *prep.* …ийн, …ын […een, …yn], …аас […ahs]
offer *n.* санал болгох [sa-nal bol-gokh]
office *n.* албан газар [al-ban ga-zar]

officer *n.* официер [ofi-tsEHr]

official *adj.* албан [al-ban]

often *adv.* байнга [bain-ga]

oil *n.* 1. тос [tos] 2. нефть [nehfti] *(as fuel)*

old *adj.* 1. хуучин [khUH-chin] *(things)* 2. хөгшин
 [khög-shin] *(person)*

on *prep.* дээр [dehr]

once *adv.* нэг удаа [neg u-dAH]

one *num.* нэг [neg]

onion *n.* сонгино [son-gi-no]

only *adj.* зөвхөн [zöv-khön]

open *adj.* нээх [nehkh]

opinion *n.* санал [sa-nal]

opportunity *n.* боломж [bo-lomj]

or *conj.* ба [ba] буюу [bu-yUH]

orange 1. *n.* жүрж [jürj] 2. *adj.* улбар шар
 [ul-bar shar] *(color)*

orange juice *n.* жүржийн ундаа [jür-jEEn un-dAH]

order 1. *n.* тушаал [tu-shAHl] 2. *v.* тушаах
 [tu-shAHkh]

organ *n.* эрхтэн [erkh-ten]

organization *n.* байгууллага [bai-gUHl-la-ga]

organize *v.* зохион байгуулах [zo-khion bai-gUH-lakh]

orphan *n.* өнчин [ön-chin]

other *adj., pron.* нөгөө [nö-gÖH]

ounce *n.* унц [unts]

our *adj.* бидний [bid-nEE]

ours *pron.* манайх [ma-naikh]

out *adv.* гадаа [ga-dAH]

outer space *n.* сансар [san-sar]

over *prep.* дээгүүр [dEH-gÜHr]

over there *adv.* наана [nah-na]

owe *v.* өртэй байх [ör-tei baikh]

owner *n.* эзэн [e-zen]

P

package *n.* илгээмж [il-gEHmj]

page *n.* хуудас [khUH-das]

pain *n.* зовиур [zo-viur]
paint *n.* будаг [bu-dag]
painter *n.* зураач [zu-rAHch], будагчин [bu-dag-chin]
painting *n.* зураг [zu-rag]
pair *n.* хос [khos]
pajamas *n.* унтлагын хувцас [unt-la-gyn khuv-tsas]
palace *n.* өргөө [ör-gÖH]
pants *n.* өмд [ömd]
paper *n.* цаас [tsahs]
pardon *n.* өршөөл [ör-shÖHl]
park *n.* цэцэрлэг [tse-tser-leg] *(recreational)*
parking *n.* зогсоол [zog-sOHl]
parliament *n.* парламент [par-lah-ment]
part *n.* хэсэг [khe-seg]
participate *v.* оролцох [o-rol-tsokh]
particular *adj.* өвөрмөц [ö-vör-möts]
party *n.* 1. нам [nam] *(polit.)* 2. үдэшлэг [ü-desh-leg]
  (social gathering)
pass 1. *n.* үнэмлэх [ü-nem-lekh] 2. *v.* дамжуулах
  [dam-jUH-lakh]
passenger *n.* зорчигч [zor-chigch]
passport *n.* паспорт [pahs-port]
past *n.* өнгөрсөн [ön-gör-söy]
patient 1. *n.* өвчтөн [övch-tön] 2. *adj.* тэсвэртэй
  [tes-ver-tei]
patronymic *n.* овог [ovog]
pay *v.* төлөх [tö-lökh]
payment *n.* төлбөр [töl-bör]
peace *n.* энх тайван [enkh tai-van]
peak *n.* оргил [or-gil]
peanut *n.* самар [sa-mar]
pearl *n.* сувд [suvd]
pedestrian *n.* явган зорчигч [yav-gan zor-chigch]
pen *n.* үзэг [ü-zeg]
penalty *n.* ял [yal]
pencil *n.* харандаа [kha-ran-dAH]
people *n.* хүмүүс [khü-mÜHs], ард [ard]
per *prep.* тутам [tu-tam]
percent *n.* хувь [khuvi]

performance *n.* тоглолт [tog-lolt]

perfume *n.* үнэртэй ус [ü-ner-tei us], духи [du-khEE]

perhaps *adv.* магадгүй [ma-gad-güi]

permit *v.* зөвшөөрөл [zöv-shÖH-röl]

person *n.* хүн [khün]

personal *adj.* хувийн [khu-vEEn]

persuade *v.* ятгах [yat-gakh]

photograph *n.* фото зураг [foh-toh zu-rag]

photographer *n.* зурагчин [zu-rag-chin]

picture *n.* зураг [zu-rag]

pie *n.* торт [tohrt]

pig *n.* гахай [ga-khai]

pillow *n.* дэр [der]

pilot *n.* нисгэгч [nis-gegch]

pine *n.* нарс [nars]

pineapple *n.* хан боргоцой [khan bor-go-tsoi]

pink *adj.* ягаан [ya-gAHn]

place *n.* байр [bair], газар [ga-zar]

plane *n.* онгоц [on-gots] *(aircraft)*

plant *n.* ургамал [ur-ga-mal] *(botanical)*

plate *n.* таваг [ta-vag]

play *v.* тоглох [tog-lokh]

pleasant *adj.* таатай [tah-tai]

plus *n.* нэмэх [ne-mekh]

p.m. *n.* үдээс хойш [ü-dEHs khoish]

pocket *n.* карман [kar-man]

poem *n.* шүлэг [shü-leg]

police *n.* цагдаа [tsag-dAH]

police officer *n.* сэргийлэгч [ser-gEE-legch]

police station *n.* цагдаагийн газар [tsag-dAH-gEEn ga-zar]

poor *adj.* ядуу [ya-dUH]

pork *n.* гахайн мах [ga-khain makh]

position *n.* байдал [bai-dal]

possible *adj.* боломжтой [bo-lomj-toi]

postcard *n.* ил захидал [il za-khi-dal]

post office *n.* шуудан [shUH-dan]

potato *n.* төмс [töms]

pound *n.* фунт [fünt]

power *n.* хүч [khüch] *(strength)*
practice *v.* давтах [dav-takh]
prefer *v.* илүү гэж үзэх [i-lÜH gej ü-zekh]
pregnant *adj.* жирэмсэн [ji-rem-sen]
preparation *n.* бэлтгэл [belt-gel]
prepare *v.* бэлтгэх [belt-gekh]
prescription *n.* жор [jor]
present 1. *n.* бэлэг [be-leg] 2. *v.* бэлэглэх [be-leg-lekh]
president *n.* ерөнхийлөгч [yö-rön-khEE-lögch]
pretty *adj.* гоё [go-yo], хөөрхөн [khÖHr-khön]
price *n.* үнэ [ü-ne]
principal 1. *n.* захирал [za-khi-ral] *(director)* 2. *adj.*
    үндсэн [ünd-sen]
printer *n.* хэвлэгч [khev-legch]
prison *n.* шорон [sho-ron]
private *adj.* хувийн [khu-vEEn]
probable *adj.* болзошгүй [bol-zosh-güi]
problem *n.* асуудал [a-sUH-dal]
procedure *n.* журам [ju-ram]
produce *v.* үйлдвэрлэх [üild-ver-lekh]
product *n.* бүтээгдэхүүн [bü-tEHg-de-khUHn]
professor *n.* профессор [pro-fes-sor]
program *n.* хөтөлбөр [khö-töl-bör]
progress *n.* хөгжил [khög-jil]
prohibit *v.* хориглох [kho-rig-lokh]
promise *v.* амлах [am-lakh]
proof *n.* нотолгоо [no-tol-gOH]
property *n.* хөрөнгө [khö-rön-gö], өмч [ömch]
protection *n.* хамгаалалт [kham-gAH-lalt]
proud *(to be)* *v.* бахархах [ba-khar-khakh]
prove *v.* батлах [bat-lakh]
public *n.* олон нийт [o-lon neet]
publish *v.* хэвлэх [khev-lekh]
punctual *adj.* нямбай [nyam-bai], цаг барьдаг
    [tsag bari-dag]
pupil *n.* сурагч [su-ragch]
purple *adj.* ягаан [ya-gAHn]
purse *n.* цүнх [tsühkh]
push *v.* түлхэх [tül-khekh]
put *v.* тавих [ta-vikh]

Q

quality *n.* чанар [cha-nar]
quantity *n.* тоо ширхэг [toh shir-kheg]
question *n.* асуулт [a-sUHlt]
quiet *adj.* тайван [tai-van], дуугай [dUH-gai]

R

radio *n.* радио [ra-dio]
railroad *n.* төмөр зам [tö-mör zam]
railroad station *n.* вокзал [vok-zAHl]
rain *n.* бороо [bo-rOH]
rainbow *n.* солонго [so-lon-go]
raincoat *n.* борооны цув [bo-rOH-ny tsuv]
raise *v.* өсгөх [ös-gökh]
raisins *n.* үзэм [ü-zem]
rapid *adj.* түргэн [tür-gen]
rare *adj.* ховор [kho-vor]
rate of exchange *n.* мөнгөний ханш [mön-gö-hEE khansh]
razor blade *n.* сахлын хутга [sakh-lyn khut-ga]
read *v.* унших [un-shikh]
ready *adj.* бэлэн болох [be-len bo-lokh]
real *adj.* жинхэнэ [jin-khe-ne]
realize *v.* ухамсарлах [u-kham-sar-lakh]
reason *n.* шалтгаан [shalt-gAHn]
receipt *n.* квитанц [kvi-tants]
receive *v.* хүлээн авах [khü-lEHn a-vakh]
recently *adj.* саяхан [saya-khan]
recognize *v.* таних [ta-nikh]
recommend *v.* санал болгох [sa-nal bol-gokh]
red *adj.* улаан [u-lAHn]
reflect *v.* сэтгэх [set-gekh]
refuse *n.* хог [khog] *(garbage)*
refuse *v.* татгалзах [tat-gal-zakh]
register *n.* бүртгэл [bürt-gel]
regular *adj.* тогтмол [togt-mol]
reindeer *n.* цаа буга [tsah bu-ga]

relatives *n.* хамаатан [kha-mAH-tan]

religion *n.* шашин [sha-shin]

rely *(on)* *v.* найдах [nai-dakh]

remain *v.* үлдэх [ül-dekh]

remember *v.* санах [sa-nakh]

remind *v.* сануулах [sa-nUH-lakh]

rent *v.* хөлслөх [khöls-lökh]

repeat *v.* дахин давтах [da-khin dav-takh]

reply *v.* хариулах [kha-riu-lakh]

report *n.* тайлан [tai-lan]

reputation *n.* нэр алдар [ner al-dar]

request *v.* гуйх [guikh], шаардагдах [shAhr-dag-dakh]

research *n.* эрэл [e-rel], судалгаа [su-dal-gAH]

reservation *n.* урьдчилан захиалга [urid-chi-lan za-khial-ga] *(hotel)*

reserve *v.* нөөцлөх [nÖHts-lökh]

resistance *n.* эсэргүүцэл [e-ser-gÜH-tsel]

respect *v.* хүндлэх [khünd-lekh]

responsibility *n.* үүрэг [ÜH-reg], хариуцлага [kha-riuts-la-ga]

responsible *adj.* үүрэгтэй [ÜH-reg-tei]

rest 1. *n.* амралт [am-ralt] 2. *v.* амрах [am-rakh]

restaurant *n.* ресторан [res-to-rAHn]

result *n.* дүн [dün]

return *v.* буцаах [bu-tsAHkh]

rice *n.* цагаан будаа [tsa-gAHn bu-dAH]

rich *adj.* баян [ba-yan]

right *n.* 1. баруун [ba-rUHn] *(direction)* 2. эрх [erkh] 3. зөв [zöv] *(correct)*

right now *adj.* яг одоо [yag o-dOH]

ring 1. *n.* бөгж [bögj] 2. *v.* утаслах [u-tas-dakh]

river *n.* гол [gol]

road *n.* зам [zam]

roast *n.* шарсан мах [shar-san makh]

rob *v.* дээрэмдэх [dEH-rem-dekh]

robber *n.* дээрэмчин [dEH-rem-chin]

room *n.* өрөө [ö-rÖH]

root *n.* үндэс [ün-des]

rose *n.* сарнай [sar-nai]

route *n.* зам [zam]

rubbish *n.* дэмий хог [de-mEE khog]
rug *n.* хивс [khivs]
rule *n.* дүрэм [dü-rem]
ruler *n.* шугам [shu-gam] *(measuring)*
run *v.* гүйх [güikh]
rush *v.* яарах [yAH-rakh]

S

sad *adj.* гунигтai [gu-nig-tai]
saddle *n.* эмээл [e-mEHl]
safe *n.* мэнд амар [mend a-mar]
salad *n.* салад [sa-lAHd]
salami *n.* хиам [khiam]
salary *n.* цалин [tsa-lin]
sale *n.* хямдрал [khyamd-ral]
salt *n.* давс [davs]
same *adj.* адил [a-dil]
sample *n.* хялбар [khyal-bar]
sandwich *n.* хачиртай талх [kha-chir-tai talkh]
satisfactory *adj.* сэтгэл ханах [set-gel kha-nakh]
Saturday *n.* бямба [byam-ba]
sauce *n.* соус [sous]
save *v.* хадгалах [khad-ga-lakh]
say *v.* хэлэх [khe-lekh]
scale 1. *n.* жин [jin] 2. *v.* жигнэх [jig-nekh]
scare *v.* айлгах [ail-gakh]
schedule *n.* цагийн хувиар [tsa-gEEn khu-viar]
school *n.* сургууль [sur-gUHli]
scientist *n.* эрдэмтэн [er-dem-ten]
scissors *n.* хайч [khaich]
sculptor *n.* уран баримал [u-ran ba-ri-mal]
sea *n.* тэнгис [ten-gis]
search *v.* хайх [khaikh]
season *n.* улирал [u-li-ral]
seat *n.* суудал [sUH-dal]
second *ord.* хоёрдугаар [kho-yor-du-gAHr]
secret *n., adj.* нууц [nuhts]
secretary *n.* нарийн бичээч [na-rEEn bi-chEHch]

section *n.* хэсэг [khe-seg]
security *n.* аюулаас хамгаалах [a-yUH-lAHs kham-gAH-lakh]
see *v.* харах [kha-rakh]
seek *v.* хайх [khaikh]
seem *v.* санагдах [sa-nag-dakh]
sell *v.* зарах [za-rakh] худалдах [khu-dal-dakh]
send *v.* явуулах [ya-vUH-lakh]
sentence *n.* өгүүлбэр [ö-gÜHl-ber] *(grammatical)*
separate 1. *adj.* тусдаа [tus-dAH] 2. *v.* салгах [sal-gakh]
servant *n.* үйлчлэгч [üilch-legch]
service *n.* үйлчилгээ [üil-chil-gEE]
seven *num.* долоо [do-lOH]
seventh *ord.* долдугаар [dol-du-gAHr]
seventy *num.* дал [dal]
several *adj.* хэд, хэдэн [khed, khe-den]
sew *v.* оёх [o-yokh]
shadow *n.* сүүдэр [sÜH-der]
share *n.* хуваалцах [khu-vAHl-tsakh]
shark *n.* цурхай загас [tsur-khai za-gas]
sharp *adj.* хурц [khurts]
shave *v.* сахал хусах [sa-khal khu-sakh]
she *pron.* тэр (эмэгтэй) [ter (e-meg-tei)]
sheep *n.* хонь [khoni]
sheepskin *n.* нэхий [ne-khEE]
sheet *n.* цагаан хэрэглэл [tsa-gAHn khe-reg-lel] *(bedding)*
shirt *n.* цамц [tsamts]
shoe *n.* гутал [gu-tal]
shop *n.* дэлгүүр [del-gÜHr]
short *adj.* богино [bo-gi-no]
shout *v.* хашгирах [khash-gi-rakh]
show 1. *n.* жүжиг [jü-jig] *(theatrical)* 2. *v.* үзүүлэх [üz-ÜHlekh]
shower *n.* шүршүүр [shür-shÜHr] *(in bathroom)*
shrimp *n.* сам хорхой [sam khor-khoi]
sick *adj.* өвчтэй [övch-tei]
sidewalk *n.* явган хүний зам [yav-gan khü-nEE zam]
sight *n.* хараа [kha-rAH] *(vision)*

sign *v.* гарын үсэг зурах [ga-ryn ü-seg zu-rakh]
signature *n.* гарын үсэг [ga-ryn ü-seg]
silk *n.* торго [tor-go]
silver *adj.* мөнгөн [mön-gön]
simple *adj.* ердийн [yör-dEEn]
since *adv.* ...аас хойш [...ahs khoish]
sing *v.* дуулах [dUH-lakh]
singer *n.* дуучин [dUH-chin]
singing *(throat) n.* хөөмий [khÖH-mEE]
single *n., adj.* ганц бие [gants bi-ye]
sink *n.* живэх [ji-vekh]
sister *n.* 1. эгч [egch] *(older)* 2. дүү [düh] *(younger)*
sit *v.* суух [suhkh]
situation *n.* байдал [bai-dal]
six *num.* зургаа [zur-gAH]
sixty *num.* жар [jar]
size *n.* размер [raz-mer], хэмжээ [khem-jEH]
skin *n.* арьс [aris]
sky *n.* тэнгэр [ten-ger]
sleep *v.* унтах [un-takh]
sleeve *n.* ханцуй [khan-tsui]
slow *adj.* удаан [u-dAHn]
small *adj.* бага [ba-ga]
smart *adj.* ухаантai [u-khAHn-tai]
smell 1. *n.* үнэр [ü-ner] 2. *v.* үнэртэх [ü-ner-tekh]
smile *n.* инээд [i-nEHd]
smoke *v.* тамхи татах [tam-khi ta-takh]
snack *n.* зууш [zuhsh]
snake *n.* могой [mo-goi]
snow *n.* цас [tsas]
soap *n.* саван [sa-van]
soup *n.* шөл [shöl]
soccer *n.* хөл бөмбөг [khöl böm-bög]
society *n.* нийгэм [nEE-gem]
socks *n.* оймс [oims]
soft *adj.* зөөлөн [zÖH-lön]
soil *n.* шороо [sho-rOH]
solve *v.* шийдэх [shEE-dekh]
some *adj.* зарим [za-rim]
someone *pron.* хэн нэгэн [khen ne-gen]

something *pron.* ямар нэгэн юм [ya-mar ne-gen yum]
sometimes *adv.* хааяа [khAH-yAH]
son *n.* хүү [khüh]
song *n.* дуу [dUH]
son-in-law *n.* хүргэн [khür-gen]
soon *adv.* удахгүй [u-dakh-güi]
sound *n.* авиа [a-via]
soup *n.* шөл [shöl]
sour cream *n.* цөцгий [tsöst-gEE]
south *n.* өмнө [öm-nö]
souvenir *n.* бэлэг дурсгал [be-leg durs-gal]
speak *v.* ярих [ya-rikh]
special *adj.* онцгой [onts-goi]
specialist *n.* мэргэжилтэн [mer-ge-jil-ten]
speech *n.* илтгэл [ilt-gel]
speed *n.* хурд [khurd]
spend *v.* зарцуулах [zar-tsUH-lakh]
spicy *adj.* халуун ногоотой [kha-lUHn no-gOH-toi]
spider *n.* аалз [AHlz]
spirit *n.* сэтгэл [set-gel]
spoon *n.* халбага [khal-ba-ga]
sport *n.* спорт [sport]
spot *n.* толбо [tol-bo]
spouse *n.* хань [khani]
spring *n.* хавар [kha-var] *(season)*
stairs *n.* шат [shat]
stamp *n.* 1. тамга [tam-ga] *(device)* 2. марк [mark]
      (postage)
start *v.* эхлэх [ekh-lekh]
state *n.* 1. муж [muj] *(administrative division)* 2. төр
      [tör] *(political)*
statement *n.* мэдээлэл [me-dEH-lel]
station *n.* зогсоол [zog-sOHl]
stationery store *n.* бичгийн дэлгүүр [bich-gEEn
      del-gÜHr]
statue *n.* хөшөө [khö-shÖH]
stay *v.* үлдэх [ül-dekh]
steak *n.* хайрсан мах [khair-san makh]
steal *v.* хулгайлах [khul-gai-lakh]
steppe *n.* хээр тал [khehr tal]

stew *n.* ЖИГНЭСЭН МАХ [jig-ne-sen makh]

still *adv.* ОДОО ХИР НЬ [o-dOH khir ni]

stockings *n.* ОЙМС [oims]

stomach *n.* ГЭДЭС [ge-des]

stomach ache *n.* ГЭДЭСНИЙ ӨВЧИН [ge-des-nEE öv-chin]

stone *n.* ЧУЛУУ [chu-lUH]

stop 1. *n.* ЗОГСООЛ [zog-sOHl] 2. *v.* ЗОГСОХ [sog-sokh]

store *n.* ДЭЛГҮҮР [del-gÜHr]

straight *adj.* ШУЛУУН [shu-lUhn]

strange *adj.* ХАЧИН [kha-chin]

strawberry *n.* ГҮЗЭЭЛЗГЭНЭ [gu-zEHlz-gene]

street *n.* ГУДАМЖ [gu-damj]

strong *adj.* ЧАДАЛТАЙ [cha-dal-tai]

structure *n.* БҮТЭЦ [bü-tets]

struggle *n.* ТЭМЦЭЛ [tem-tsel]

student *n.* ОЮУТАН [o-yUH-tan]

study *v.* СУРАХ [su-rakh], СУДЛАХ [sud-lakh]

style *n.* МАЯГ [ma-yag]

subtract *v.* ХАСАХ [kha-sakh]

subtraction *n.* ХАСАХ ҮЙЛДЭЛ [kha-sakh üil-del]

success *n.* АМЖИЛТ [am-jilt]

such *adj., pron.* ТИЙМ НЭГ [tEEm neg]

suddenly *adv.* ГЭНЭТ [ge-net]

sugar *n.* СААХАР [sAH-khar]

suit 1. *n.* КОСТЮМ [kos-tyum] 2. *v.* ТААРАХ [tAH-rakh]

sum *n.* НИЙЛБЭР [nEEl-ber]

summarize *v.* ДҮГНЭЛТ [düg-nelt]

summer *n.* ЗУН [zun]

sun *n.* НАР [nar]

Sunday *n.* НЯМ [nyam]

sure *adj.* БАТТАЙ [bat-tai]

surgery *n.* МЭС ЗАСАЛ [mes za-sal]

swear *v.* ТАНГАРАГЛАХ [tan-ga-rag-lakh]

sweat 1. *n.* ХӨЛС [khöls] 2. *v.* ХӨЛРӨХ [khöl-rökh]

sweater *n.* НООСОН ЦАМЦ [nOH-son tsamts]

sweet *adj.* ЧИХЭРЛЭГ [chi-kher-leg]

sweetheart *n.* АМРАГ [am-rag]

swim *v.* СЭЛЭХ [se-lekh]

swimming pool *n.* БАССЕЙН [bas-sein]

T

table *n.* ширээ [shi-rEH]
tail *n.* сүүл [sühl]
take *v.* авах [a-vakh]
take care of *v.* халамжлах [kha-lamj-lakh]
tale *n.* домог [do-mog]
talk *v.* ярих [ya-rikh]
tall *adj.* өндөр [ön-dör]
taste *n.* амт [amt]
tasty *adj.* амттай [amt-tai]
tax *n.* татвар [tat-var]
taxi *n.* такси [tak-si]
tea *n.* цай [tsai]
tea party *n.* цайллага [tsail-la-ga]
teach *v.* заах [zAHkh]
teacher *n.* багш [bagsh]
team *n.* баг [bag]
tear *n.* нулимс [nu-lims]
technical *adj.* техникийн [tekh-ni-kEEn]
technology *n.* техник [tekh-nik]
telegram *n.* цахилгаан [tsa-khil-gAHn]
telephone *n.* утас [u-tas]
television *n.* телевиз [te-le-vEEz]
ten *num.* арав [a-rav]
tennis *n.* теннис [ten-nis]
tent *n.* майхан [mai-khan]
terrible *adj.* аймшигт [aim-shigt]
test *n.* шүүлэг [shÜH-leg], шалгалт [shal-galt]
than *conj.* ...аас [...ahs]
Thank you. *coll.* Баярлалаа! [ba-yar-la-lAH]
That's it! *coll.* Ингээд л болоо [in-gEHd l bo-lOH]
the *art. There is no definite article in Mongolian.*
theater *n.* театр [te-yatr]
their *adj.* тэдний [ted-nEE]
then *adv.* тэгээд [te-gEHd]
there *adv.* тэнд [tend]
they *pron.* тэд [ted]
thief *n.* хулгайч [khul-gaich]
thin *adj.* нимгэн [nim-gen]

thing *n.* юм [yum]
think *v.* бодох [bo-dokh]
third *ord.* гуравдугаар [gu-rav-du-gAHr]
thirsty *(to be) v.* цангах [tsan-gakh]
thirteen *num.* арван гурав [ar-van gu-rav]
thirty *num.* гуч [guch]
this *adj.* энэ [e-ne]
thousand *num.* мянга [myan-ga]
three *num.* гурав [gu-rav]
throat *n.* хоолой [khOH-loi]
throw *v.* хаях [kha-yakh]
Thursday *n.* пүрэв [pü-rev]
ticket *n.* тасалбар [ta-sal-bar]
tie *n.* зангиа [zan-gia]
tiger *n.* бар [bar]
time *n.* хугацаа [khu-ga-tsAH]
tip *n.* гар цайлгах [gar tsail-gakh] *(money)*
tire *n.* дугуй [du-gui]
tired *(to be) adj.* ядарсан [ya-dar-san]
to *prep.* руу [ruh] рүү [rüh]
tobacco *n.* тамхи [tam-khi]
today *adv.* өнөөдөр [ö-nÖH-dör]
toe *n.* хөлийн хуруу [khö-lEEn khu-rUH]
together *adv.* хамт [khamt]
toilet *n.* жорлон [jor-lon]
toll *n.* замын хураамж [za-myn khu-rAHmj]
tomato *n.* улаан лооль [u-lAHn lOHli]
tomorrow *adv.* маргааш [mar-gAHsh]
tongue *n.* хэл [khel]
tonight *n., adv.* өнөө шөнө [ö-nÖH shö-nö]
too *adv.* бас [bas]
too much *adv.* маш их [mash ikh]
tool *n.* багаж [ba-gaj]
tooth *n.* шүд [shüd]
toothache *n.* шүд өвдөх [shüd öv-dökh]
toothpaste *n.* оо [oh]
total *adj.* нийт дүн [nEEt dün]
tourism *n.* жуулчлал [jUHlch-lal]
tourist *n.* жуулчин [jUHl-chin]
towel *n.* гарын алчуур [ga-ryn al-chUHr]

town *n.* ХОТ [khot]
toy *n.* ТОГЛООМ [tog-lOHm]
trade *n.* худалдаа [khu-dal-dAH]
tradition *n.* ёс заншил [yos zan-shil]
traffic *n.* замын хөдөлгөөн [za-myn khö-döl-gÖHn]
train *n.* галт тэрэг [galt te-reg]
translate *v.* орчуулах [or-chUH-lakh]
translation *n.* орчуулга [or-chUHl-ga]
translator *n.* орчуулагч [or-chUH-lagch]
transportation *n.* ТЭЭВЭР [tEH-ver]
trash *n.* ХОГ [khog]
travel *v.* ЗОРЧИХ [zor-chikh]
treasure *n.* эрдэнэ [er-de-ne]
treat *v.* анагаах [a-na-gAHkh]
treatment *n.* эмчилгээ [em-chil-gEH]
tree *n.* МОД [mod]
trip *n.* аялал [a-ya-lal]
trousers *n.* ӨМД [ömd]
truck *n.* ачааны машин [a-chAH-ny ma-shin]
true *adj.* ҮНЭН [ü-nen]
trunk *n.* авдар [av-dar] *(chest)*
truth *n.* ҮНЭН [ü-nen]
try *v.* ОРОЛДОХ [o-rol-dokh], ХИЧЭЭХ [khi-chEHkh]
try on *v.* ОРОЛДОХ [o-rol-dokh]
Tuesday *n.* МЯГМАР [myag-mar]
turn 1. *n.* ЭЭЛЖ [ehlj] 2. *v.* ЭРГЭХ [er-gekh]
turn off *v.* унтраах [unt-rAHkh]
turn on *v.* асаах [a-sAHkh]
twelve *num.* арван хоёр [ar-van kho-yor]
twenty *num.* ХОРЬ [khori]
two *num.* ХОЁР [kho-yor]
typical *adj.* НИЙТЛЭГ [nEEt-leg]

U

ugly *adj.* ЗЭВҮҮН МУУХАЙ [ze-vÜHn mUH-khai]
umbrella *n.* нарны халх [nar-ny khalkh]
uncle *n.* авга [av-ga]
uncomfortable *adj.* ТАВГҮЙ [tav-güi]

under *prep.* ДООР [dohr]
underneath *adv.* ДООР НЬ [dohr ni]
understand *v.* ОЙЛГОХ [oil-gokh]
understanding *n.* ОЙЛГОЛТ [oil-golt]
underwear *n.* ДОТООЖ [do-tOHj]
union *n.* ЭВЛЭЛ [ev-lel]
unite *v.* НЭГДЭХ [neg-dekh]
university *n.* ИХ СУРГУУЛЬ [ikh sur-gUHli]
unless *conj.* ХЭРЭВ …ГҮЙ БОЛ [khe-rev …güi bol]
unmarried *adj.* ГЭРЛЭЭГҮЙ [ger-lEH-güi]
unnecessary *adj.* ХЭРЭГГҮЙ [khe-reg-güi]
unoccupied *adj.* ЧӨЛӨӨТЭЙ [chö-lÖH-tei], ХООСОН [khOH-son]
unpleasant *adj.* ТААГҮЙ [tAH-gui]
until *prep.* ХҮРТЭЛ [khür-tel]
up *adv.* ӨӨД [öhd], ДЭЭШ [dehsh]
upstairs *adj.* ДЭЭД ДАВХАР [dEHd dav-khar]
urban *adj.* ХОТЫН [kho-tyn]
urgent *adj.* ЯАРАЛТАЙ [yAH-ral-tai]
us *pron.* БИД [bid], БИДЭНД [bi-dend]
use *v.* ХЭРЭГЛЭХ [khe-reg-lekh]
useful *adj.* ХЭРЭГТЭЙ [khe-reg-tei]
usual *adj.* ЕРИЙН [ye-rEEn]

V

vacancy *n.* СУЛ [sul], ХООСОН [khOH-son]
vaccine *n.* ВАКЦИН [vak-tsin]
valid *adj.* ХҮЧИН ТӨГӨЛДӨР [khü-chin tö-göl-dör]
valley *n.* ХЭЭР ТАЛ [khehr tal]
valuable *adj.* ҮНЭТ [ü-net]
value *n.* ҮНЭ ЦЭНЭ [ü-ne tse-ne]
vanilla *n.* ВАНИЛИН [va-ni-lin]
various *adj.* ЯНЗ ЯНЗЫН [yanz yan-zyn]
vase *n.* ВААР [vahr]
veal *n.* ТУГАЛЫН МАХ [tu-ga-lyn makh]
vegetable *n.* НОГОО [no-gOH]
vegetarian *n.* ЦАГААН ХООЛТОН [tsa-gAHn khOHl-ton]
very *adv.* МАШ [mash], ХАМГИЙН [kham-gEEn]

view *n.* харагдац [kha-rag-dats]
visa *n.* виз [viz]
visit *v.* айлчлах [ailch-lakh]
visitor *n.* айлчин [ail-chin]
vitamin *n.* витамин [vi-ta-mEEn]
vodka *n.* архи [ar-khi]
voice *n.* дуу хоолой [duh khOH-loi]
volleyball *n.* волейбол [vo-lei-bOHl]

W

wages *n.* цалин [tsa-lin]
wait *v.* хүлээх [khü-lEHkh]
waiter/waitress *n.* зөөгч [zöhgch]
wake up *v.* сэрэх [se-rekh]
walk 1. *n.* алхаа [al-khAH] 2. *v.* алхах [al-khakh]
wall *n.* хана [kha-na]
wallet *n.* түрийвч [tü-rEEvch]
want *v.* хүсэх [khü-sekh]
war *n.* дайн [dain]
warm *adj.* дулаан [du-lAHn]
watch 1. *n.* цаг [tsag] (time piece) 2. *v.* үзэх [ü-zekh]
watchman *n.* манаач [ma-nAHch]
water *n.* ус [us]
watermelon *n.* шийгуа [shEE-gua]
we *pron.* бид [bid]
weak *adj.* дорой [do-roi], сул [sul]
wealth *n.* баялаг [ba-ya-lag]
weapon *n.* зэвсэг [zev-seg]
wear *v.* өмсөх [öm-sökh]
weary *adj.* ядарсан [ya-dar-san]
weather *n.* цаг агаар [tsag a-gAHr]
wedding *n.* хурим [khu-rim]
Wednesday *n.* лхагва [l-khag-va]
week *n.* долоо хоног [do-lOH kho-nog]
weight *n.* жин [jin]
welcome *adj.* таатай [tAH-tai]
Welcome to ... *coll.* ...д тавтай морилно уу
    [...d tav-tai mo-ril-no uh]

well *adj.* сайн [sain]
well done *adj.* гүйцэд болгосон [güi-tsed bol-go-son]
west *n.* өрнө [ör-nö]
what *adv.* ямар [ya-mar]
whatever *adj.* ямар ч [ya-mar ch]
wheel *n.* жолоо [jo-lOH]
when *adv.* хэзээ[khe-zEH], хэдийд [khe-dEEd]
where *adv.* хаана [khAH-na]
while *conj.* хоорон [khOH-rond]
whisky *n.* виски [wisky]
white *adj.* цагаан [tsa-gAHn]
who *pron.* хэн [khen]
whole *adj.* бүтэн [bü-ten]
why *interr.* яагаад [yAH-gAHd]
wide *adj.* өргөн [ör-gön]
width *n.* өргөн [ör-gön]
wife *n.* эхнэр [ekh-ner], гэргий [ger-gEE]
wild *adj.* зэрлэг [zer-leg]
win *v.* ялах [ya-lakh]
wind *n.* салхи [sal-khi]
window *n.* цонх [tsonkh]
wine *n.* дарс [dars]
winter *n.* өвөл [ö-völ]
wish *v.* хүсэх [khü-sekh]
witchcraft *n.* илбэ [il-be]
with *prep.* ...тай хамт [...tai khamt]
without *prep.* ...үгүй [... ü-güi]
woman *n.* эмэгтэй хүн [e-meg-tei khün], хүүхэн [khÜH-khen]
wood *n.* ой мод [oi mod]
wool *n.* ноос [nohs]
word *n.* үг [üg]
work *n.* ажил [a-jil]
world *n.* дэлхий [del-khEE], ертөнц [yör-tönts]
worry *v.* санаа зовох [sa-nAH zo-vokh]
worse *adj.* хамгийн муу [kham-gEEn muh]
worth *n.* үнэ [ü-ne]
write *v.* бичих [bi-chikh]
writer *n.* зохиолч [zo-khiolch]
wrong *adj.* буруу [bu-rUH]

X

X ray *n.* рентген зураг [rent-gen zu-rag]

Y

yak *n.* сарлаг [sar-lag]
year *n.* жил [jil]
yearly *adj.* жил тутмын [jil tut-myn]
yellow *adj.* шар [shar]
yes *adv.* за [za], тийм [tEEm]
yesterday *adv.* өчигдөр [ö-chig-dör]
yet *adv.* бас [bas], атал [a-tal]
you *pron.* чи [chi], та [ta]
young *adj.* залуу [za-lUH]
your *adj.* чиний [chi-nEE]
yours *pron.* чинийх [chi-nEEkh]
youth *n.* идэр нас [i-der nas]

Z

zero *n.* тэг [teg]
zipper *n.* цахилгаан [tsa-khil-gAHn]
zone *n.* бүс нутаг [büs nu-tag]
zoo *n.* зоо парк [zoh park]

MONGOLIAN PHRASEBOOK

Greetings and Basic Phrases

Hello! Hi!
Сайн байна уу?
[sain bain uh]

How have you been?
Амар байна уу?
[a-mar bain uh]

Good morning!
Өглөөний мэнд!
[ög-lÖH-nEE mend]

Good afternoon!
Өдрийн мэнд!
[öd-rEEn mend]

Good evening!
Оройн мэнд!
[o-roin mend]

Good night!
Сайхан нойрсоорой!
[sai-khan noir-sOH-roi]

How are you?
Та сайн уу?
[ta sain uh]

Fine, thanks.
Сайн, баярлалаа.
[sain, ba-yar-la-lAH]

And you?
Харин та?
[kha-rin ta]

What's new?
Сонин юутай байна?
[so-nin yUH-tai bain]

Nothing.
Юмгүй ээ.
[yum-güi eh]

My name is …
Миний нэр…
[mi-nEE ner …]

What is your name?
Таны нэрийг хэн гэдэг вэ?
[ta-ny ne-rEEg khen ge-deg ve]

I'm John.
Би Жон.
[bi John]

I'd like to introduce you to …
Би таныг … тай танилцуулья.
[bi ta-nyg … tai ta-nil-tsUHl-ya]

Nice to meet you.
Таатай байна.
[tAH-tai bain]

What is the weather like?
Цаг агаар ямар байна?
[tsag a-gAHr ya-mar bain]

The weather is fine.
Тэнгэр сайхан байна.
[ten-ger sai-khan bain]

The weather is bad.
Тэнгэр муухай байна.
[ten-ger mUH-khai bain]

Greetings and Basic Phrases

It's hot.
Халуун байна.
[kha-lUHn bain]

It's cold.
Хүйтэн байна.
[khüi-ten bain]

I'm hot.
Би халууцаж байна.
[bi kha-lUH-tsaj bain]

I'm cold.
Би даарч байна.
[bi dAHr-ch bain]

Thank you!
Баярлалаа!
[ba-yar-la-lAH]

Thank you very much!
Их баярлалаа!
[ikh ba-yar-la-lAH]

Don't mention it!
Зүгээр!
[zü-gEHr]

It was nice meeting you.
Тантай танилцахад таатай байлаа
[tan-tai ta-nil-tsa-khad tAH-tai bai-lAH]

Take it easy!
Сайхан амраарай!
[sai-khan am-rAH-rai]

See you again!
Дахин уулзатлаа баяртай!
[da-khin UHlz-tlAH ba-yar-tai]

Goodbye! Bye!
   Баяртай!
   [ba-yar-tai]

Names

patronymic
   овог
   [o-vog]

given name
   өөрийн нэр
   [ÖHr-EEn ner]

There is no surname in Mongolian directly equivalent to American usage. Mongolians use two names: the first of these is based on the father's name (patronymic), to which is added an adjectival suffix (-een, -yn). This name is followed by what could properly be called the given name, that is, the name most often used. In the example Bat-yn Oyuunjargal, the father's given name is Bat, and his child's name is Oyuunjargal.

A Mongolian's given name consists of two or three names. Quite popular names are Altan (golden), Naran (sun), Saran (moon), Baatar (hero), Bat (strong), Chuluun (stone), Bold (steel), Tsetseg (flower), Bolor (crystal), Saikhan (beauty), Erdene (treasure), Enkh (piece), Jargal (happiness), Oyuun (turquoise), Gerel (light), and these names are frequently combined: Altangerel, Narantsetseg, etc.

Short or pet forms of given names are used within the family or among close friends. After marriage a woman preserves her maiden name.

What is your name?
   Чиний нэрийг хэн гэдэг вэ?
   [chi-nEE ne-rEEg khen ge-deg ve]

Greetings and Basic Phrases

What is your name? (deferential)
   Таны нэрийг хэн гэдэг вэ?
   [ta-ny ne-rEEg khen ge-deg ve]

My name is Saran. (full form)
   Миний нэрийг Саран гэдэг.
   [mi-nEE ne-rEEg sa-ran ge-deg]

My name is Saran. (short form)
   Миний нэр Саран.
   [mi-nEE ner sa-ran]

What is your patronymic?
   Чиний овгийг хэн гэдэг вэ?
   [chi-nEE ov-rEEg khen ge-deg ve]

My patronymic is Dorj.
   Миний овгийг дорж гэдэг.
   [mi-nEE ov-gEEg dorj ge-deg]

My patronymic is Dorj.
   Миний овог Дорж.
   [mi-nEE ovog dorj]

What is your full name?
   Таны овог нэрийг хэн гэдэг вэ?
   [ta-ny o-vog ne-rEEg khen ge-deg ve]

My full name is Dorjiin Saran.
   Миний овог нэр Доржийн Саран.
   [mi-nEE o-vog ner dor-jEEn sa-ran]

I'm Dorjiin Saran.
   Би Доржийн Саран.
   [bi dor-jEEn sa-ran]

I'm Saran.
   Би Саран.
   [bi sa-ran]

Forms of address

When addressing each other, Mongolians use names, relationships or job titles. The polite form of direct address is formed by adding double long vowels after the names. The deferential form of "Mr." and "Mrs." is the word *guai*.

Bayar aa!
  Баяр аа!
  [ba-yar AH]

Tsetseg ee!
  Цэцэг ээ!
  [tse-tseg EH]

Mr. Bayar!
  Баяр гуай!
  [ba-yar guai]

Mrs./Ms./Miss Tsetseg!
  Цэцэг гуай!
  [tse-tse-gEH guai]

Dad!
  Аав аа!
  [AHv AH]

Mom!
  Ээж ээ!
  [EHj EH]

When Mongolians address non-Mongolians, they use two special words: *noyon* ["Mr."] in reference to males, and *khatagtai* ["Mrs.", "Ms.", "Miss"] in reference to females.

Mr. Jones!
  Ноён Жонс!
  [no-yon Jones]

Mrs./Ms./Miss Jones
    Хатагтай Жонс!
    [kha-tag-tai Jones]

Ladies and Gentlemen!
    Ноёд хатагтай нар аа!
    [no-yod kha-tag-tai nar AH]

You can address people by their profession:

Boss!
    Дарга аа!
    [dar-ga AH]

Driver!
    Жолооч оо!
    [jo-lOHch OH]

Doctor!
    Эмч ээ!
    [emch EH]

Nurse!
    Сувилагч аа!
    [su-vi-lagch AH]

Waiter!
    Зөөгч өө!
    [zöhgch ÖH]

Officer!
    Цагдаа!
    [tsag-dAH]

Operator!
    Залгагч аа!
    [zal-gagch AH]

In Mongolian, if somebody calls you Ах аа! [akh AH] "Brother!" or Эгч ээ! [egch EH] "Sister!" don't be surprised. It is a common form of address and often refers to older people.

Age

How old are you? (informal)
Чи хэдэн настай вэ?
[chi khe-den nas-tai ve]

How old are you? (formal)
Та хэдэн настай вэ?
[ta khe-den nas-tai ve]

How old are you? (plural)
Та нар хэдэн настай вэ?
[ta nar khe-den nas-tai ve]

I'm thirty years old.
Би гучин настай.
[bi gu-chin nas-tai]

But you look so young.
Та залуу харагдаж байна.
[ta za-lUH kha-rag-daj bain]

How old is John?
Жон хэдэн настай вэ?
[John khe-den nas-tai ve]

John is ten years old.
Жон арван настай.
[John ar-van nas-tai] *or*

Ten
Аравтай.
[a-rav-tai]

Greetings and Basic Phrases

Requests

What time is it?
Хэдэн цаг болж байна вэ?
[khe-den tsag bolj bain ve]

How do I get to..., please?
... руу яаж очихыг хэлж өгнө үү?
[... ruh yAHj o-chi-khyg khelj ög-nö üh]

When can I have an appointment?
Хэзээ таньтай уулзаж болох вэ?
[khe-zEH tani-tai UHl-zaj bo-lokh ve]

Could you help me?
Надад туслана уу?
[na-dad tus-la-na uh]

Could you do me a favor?
Та надад тус болно уу?
[ta na-dad tus bol-no uh]

Response

Certainly. Of course.
Тэгье. Тэгэлгүй яахав!
[tegi-ye. te-gel-güi yAH-khav]

Yes.
За. Тийм.
[za teem]

I'm sorry. No.
Уучлаарай. Үгүй.
[UHch-lAH-rai. ü-güi]

Greetings and Basic Phrases

Expressing gratitude

Thank you!
Баярлалаа!
[ba-yar-la-lAH]

Thank you very much!
Их баярлалаа!
[ikh ba-yar-la-lAH]

I'm very grateful to you!
Танд талархаж байна!
[tand ta-lar-khaj bain]

Response

You're welcome.
Зүгээр.
[zu-gEHr]

It was a pleasure.
Надад таатай байна.
[na-dad tAH-tai bain]

Agreement

I agree.
Би зөвшөөрч байна.
[bi zöv-shÖH-rch bain]

I completely agree.
Би дуртai зөвшөөрч байна.
[bi dur-tai zöv-shÖH-rch bain]

You're right.
Таны зөв.
[ta-ny zöv]

I think so too.
> Би бас тэгэж бодож байна.
> [bi bas te-gej bo-doj bain]

I can see your point.
> Би таныг ойлгож байна.
> [bi ta-nyg oil-goj bain]

That is a good idea.
> Энэ их сайхан санаа байна.
> [e-ne ikh sai-khan sa-nAH bain]

Sure!
> Тэгье!
> [tegi-ye]

Fine!
> Сайн байна!
> [sain bain]

Disagreement

I don't agree.
> Би зөвшөөрөхгүй.
> [bi zöv-shÖH-rökh-güi]

I don't think so.
> Би тэгэж бодохгүй байна.
> [bi te-gej bo-dokh-güi bain]

I think you are wrong.
> Таны буруу гэж бодож байна.
> [ta-ny bu-rUH gej bo-doj bain]

I cannot.
> Би чадахгүй.
> [bi cha-dakh-güi]

It is not possible.
Болохгүй.
[bo-lokh-güi]

No. Not.
Үгүй.
[ü-güi]

Apologies

Excuse me. (I'm sorry.)
Уучлаарай.
[uhch-lAH-rai]

That is all right.
Зүгээр.
[zü-gEHr]

That is my fault.
Энэ миний буруу.
[e-ne mi-nEE bu-rUH]

That is my mistake.
Энэ миний алдаа.
[e-ne mi-nEE al-dAH]

Don't worry.
Санаа зоволтгүй.
[sa-nAH zo-volt-güi]

I'm sorry. I don't understand you.
Уучлаарай. Би таныг ойлгосонгүй
[UHch-lAH-rai. bi ta-nyg oil-go-son-güi]

Can you spell it?
Үсэглэж хэлж өгнө үү?
[ü-seg-lej khelj ög-nö üh]

Greetings and Basic Phrases

Congratulations and Exclamations

Congratulations!
> Баяр хүргэе!
> [ba-yar khür-ge-ye]

Thank you, the same to you.
> Баярлалаа, таньд ч бас.
> [ba-yar-la-lAH, tanid ch bas]

Happy birthday!
> Төрсөн өдрийн мэнд хүргэе!
> [tör-sön öd-rEEn mend xür-ge-ye]

Happy holiday!
> Баярын мэнд хүргэе!
> [ba-yar-yn mend khür-ge-ye]

Happy New Year!
> Шинэ жилийн мэнд хүргэе!
> [shi-ne ji-lEEn mend xür-ge-ye]

Merry Christmas!
> Зул сарын мэнд хүргэе!
> [zul sa-ryn mend xür-ge-ye]

Well-wishing

Good luck!
> Амжилт хүсье!
> [am-jilt khüsi-ye]

Enjoy yourself!
> Сайхан амраарай!
> [sai-khan am-rAH-rai]

All the best!
> Сайн сайхныг хүсье!
> [sain saikh-nyg khüsi-ye]

Greetings and Basic Phrases

Enjoy your meal!
Сайхан хооллоорой!
[sai-khan khOHl-lOH-roi]

Have a good trip!
Сайн яваарай!
[sain ya-vAH-rai]

Time expressions

What time is it?
Хэдэн цаг болж байна?
[khe-den tsag bolj bain]

It's one o'clock.
Нэг цаг болж байна.
[neg tsag bolj bain]

It's three o'clock.
Гурван цаг болж байна.
[gur-van tsag bolj bain]

It's half past two.
Хоёр хагас болж байна.
[kho-yor kha-gas bolj bain]

It's ten to four.
Дөрөвт арав дутуу байна.
[dö-rövt a-rav du-tUH bain]

It's a quarter of six.
Зургаа арван тав болж байна.
[zur-gAH ar-van tav bolj bain]

What's today's date?
Өнөөдрийн он сар хэдэн вэ?
[ö-nÖHd-rEEn on sar khe-den ve]

Greetings and Basic Phrases

The tenth of March
Гурван сарын арван
[gur-van sa-ryn ar-van]

yesterday
өчигдөр
[ö-chig-dör]

today
өнөөдөр
[ö-nÖH-dör]

tomorrow
маргааш
[mar-gAHsh]

the day before yesterday
уржигдар
[ur-jig-dar]

the day after tomorrow
нөгөөдөр
[nö-gÖH-dör]

two days (weeks, months)
хоёр өдөр (долоо хоног, сар)
[kho-yor ö-dÖr (do-lOH kho-nog, sar)]

in an hour
нэг цагийн дараа
[neg tsa-gEEn da-rAH]

in the morning
өглөөд
[ög-lÖHd]

in the evening
оройд
[o-roid]

in the afternoon
ҮДЭЭС ХОЙШ
[ü-dEHs khoish]

at night
шөнөдөө
[shö-nö-dÖH]

on Tuesday
Мягмарт
[myag-mart]

a week from Tuesday
Мягмараас 1 долоо хоног
[myag-ma-rAHs neg do-lOH kho-nog]

now
одоо
[o-dOH]

then
тэр үед
[ter ü-yed]

this year (month)
энэ онд (сард)
[e-ne ond (sard)]

this week
энэ долоо хоногт
[e-ne do-lOH kho-nogt]

last year (month)
өнгөрсөн жил (сар)
[ön-gör-sön jil (sar)]

last week
өнгөрсөн долоо хоногт
[ön-gör-sön do-lOH kho-nogt]

next year (month)
    ирэх жил (сар)
    [i-rekh jil (sar)]

next week
    ирэх долоо хоногт
    [i-rekh do-lOH kho-nogt]

about seven
    долоон цагийн орчим
    [do-lOH tsa-gEEn or-chim]

by seven
    долоо гэхэд
    [do-lOH ge-khed]

after seven
    долоогоос хойш
    [do-lOH-gOHs khoish]

before seven
    долоогоос өмнө
    [do-lOH-gOHs öm-nö]

from six till seven
    зургаагаас долоон цагийн хооронд
    [zur-gAH-gAHs do-lOHn tsa-gEEn khOH-rond]

early
    эрт
    [ert]

late
    оройтон
    [o-roi-ton]

on time
    яг цагтаа
    [yag tsag-tAH]

Transportation

The international Mongolian air carrier is MIAT (Монг, олын Иргэний Агаарын Тээвэр) [mon-go-lyn ir-ge-nEE a-gAH-ryn tEH-ver].

MIAT offers scheduled and chartered services to all domestic airports as well as overseas destinations such as Moscow, Beijing, Berlin, Osaka, Seoul, Irkutsk, Hong Kong, Hoh-Hot (Inner Mongolia) and Almaty (Kazakhstan). Ulaanbaatar's international airport, Buyant Ukhaa, is located in the southwestern part of the capital. Tickets can also be purchased at MIAT's downtown ticket office in Ulaanbaatar located two blocks west of Sukhbaatar Square. Mongolian aircraft include the Airbus A310, Boeing 727, Antonov AN24, AN-2 and MI-8 helicopters. Helicopters are available for flights to the Mongolian countryside. Mongolian Airlines has representatives in Moscow, Beijing, Berlin, Tokyo, Seoul, Hoh-Hot and Irkutsk.

When you arrive at Buyant Ukhaa some airport employees will speak English, but to avoid any unpleasantness, some helpful phrases are as follows:

I've arrived on flight OM 226.
   Би ОM 226-гаар ирсэн.
   [bi OM kho-yor zuhn kho-rin zur-gAH-gAHr irsen]

I'm ...
   Би ... хүн.
   [bi ... khün]

   ... American.
      ... Америка ...
      [a-mEH-ri-ka]

   ... Australian.
      ... Австрали ...
      [avs-trAH-li]

... English.
... Англи ...
[AHng-li]

Here is my passport.
Энэ миний пасспорт.
[e-ne mi-nEE pas-port]

I'm ...
Би ...
[bi...]

    ... an engineer.
    ...инженер.
    [in-je-nEHr]

    ... a doctor.
    ... эмч.
    [emch]

    ... a teacher.
    ... багш.
    [bagsh]

    ... a tourist.
    ... жуулчин.
    [jUHl-chin]

I'm here on ...
Би ... яваа.
[bi ...ya-vAH]

    ... a personal visit
    ... хувиараа
    [khu-via-rAH]

    ... business
    ... ажлаар
    [aj-lAHr]

I've come to visit friends.

    Би найзындаа айлчлахаар ирсэн.

    [bi nai-zyn-dAH ailch-la-khAHr ir-sen]

The visa was issued by the Mongolian Embassy in America.

    Визийг Америка дахь Монголын Элчин

        Сайдын Яамнаас авсан.

    [vi-zEEg a-me-ri-ka da-khi mon-go-lyn el-chin

        sai-dyn yAHm-nAHs av-san]

The visa is good for six months.

    Виз зургаан сарын хүчинтэй.

    [viz zur-gAHn sa-ryn xü-chin-tei]

I don't know exactly how long I'll be here.

    Би хир удахаа мэдэхгүй байна.

    [bi xir u-da-khAH me-dekh-güi bain]

My address in Mongolia is …

    Миний Монголд байх хаяг …

    [mi-nEE mon-gold baikh kha-yag]

I'm alone.

    Би ганцаараа яваа.

    [bi gan-tsAH-rAH ya-vAH]

I'm with my wife (husband) and my child.

    Би эхнэр (нөхөр) хүүхэдтэйгээ яваа.

    [bi ekh-ner (nö-khör) khÜH-khed-tei-gEH ya-vAH]

Baggage claim

Where is the baggage claim area?

    Ачаагаа хаанаас авах вэ?

    [a-chAH-gAH khAH-nAHs avakh ve]

Where can I get a baggage cart?

    Ачааны түрдэг тэрэг хаанаас авах вэ?

    [a-chAH-ny tür-deg te-reg khAH-nAHs avakh ve]

All baggage from flight number … has already arrived, but my luggage isn't there.

… номерийн нислэгийн бүх ачаа ирсэн ч миний ачаа алга.

[no-me-rEEn nis-le-gEEn bükh a-chAH ir-sen ch mi-nEE a-chAH al-ga]

My suitcase is lost.

Миний чемодан алга байна.

[mi-nEE che-mo-dAHn al-ga bain]

My suitcase is damaged.

Миний чемодан эвдэрсэн байна.

[mi-nEE che-mo-dAHn ev-der-sen bain]

Who can I see about it?

Би энэ тухай хэнтэй уулзах вэ?

[bi e-ne tu-khai khen-tei UHl-zakh ve]

I've left my briefcase on the plane. How can I get it?

Би онгоцонд цүнхээ мартсан байна. Яаж авах вэ?

[bi on-go-tsong tsün-khEH mart-san bain. yAHj a-akh ve]

I've lost my baggage claim check.

Би ачааны бичгээ гээсэн байна.

[bi a-chAh-ny bich-gEH gEH-sen bain]

Customs

Where can I get a declaration form?

Би мэдүүлэг хаанаас авах вэ?

[bi me-dÜH-leg khAH-nAHs a-vakh ve]

I've come with my family.

Би гэр бүлээрээ ирсэн.

[bi ger bü-lEH-rEH ir-sen]

Is it necessary for each member of my family to fill out
a separate form?
> Манай гэр бүлийнхэн тус тусдаа бөглөх
> ёстой юу?
> [ma-nai ger bü-lEEn-khen tus tus-dAH bög-lökh
> yos-toi yUH]

What do I write here?
> Энд юу бичих вэ?
> [end yUH bi-chikh ve]

Where must I sign?
> Гарын үсгээ хаана зурах вэ?
> [ga-ryn üs-gEH khAH-na zu-rakh ve]

Here is my declaration.
> Энэ миний гаалийн мэдүүлэг.
> [e-ne mi-nEE gAH-lEEn me-dÜH-leg]

Here are my things.
> Энэ миний юмнууд.
> [e-ne mi-nEE yum-nUHd]

This is all my luggage.
> Энэ миний бүх ачаа.
> [e-ne mi-nEE bükh a-chAH]

I've got a lot of luggage.
> Би их ачаатай.
> [bi ikh a-chAH-tai]

I have nothing else.
> Надад өөр юм байхгүй.
> [na-dad öhr yum baikh-güi]

There are no prohibited items in my luggage.
> Надад хориотой юм байхгүй.
> [na-dad kho-rio-toi yum baikh-güi]

Should I open my suitcase?
Би чемоданаа онгойлгох уу?
[bi che-mo-dAH-nAH on-goil-gokh uh]

May I close my bag?
Би чемоданаа хааж болох уу?
[bi che-mo-dAH-nAH khaaj bo-lokh uh]

These are my personal belongings.
Энд миний хувийн юмнууд байгаа.
[end mi-nEE khu-vEEn yum-nUHd bai-gAH]

I have some small presents for my friends.
Би найз нартаа өгөх жаахан бэлэгтэй.
[bi naiz nar-tAH ö-gökh jAH-khan be-leg-tei]

These are souvenirs.
Энд бэлэг дурсгалын зүйлс байгаа.
[end be-leg durs-ga-lyn züils bai-gAH]

I have ... dollars.
Надад ... доллар байгаа.
[na-dad ... dOHl-lar bai-gAH]

Must I show that amount on the declaration?
Энийг гаалийн мэдүүлэгт бичих үү?
[e-nEEg gAh-lEEn me-dÜH-legt bi-chikh üh]

I have no Mongolian money.
Надад Монгол мөнгө байхгүй.
[na-dad mon-gol mön-gö baikh-güi]

Where can I change money?
Мөнгөө хаана солиулах вэ?
[mön-gÖH khAH-na so-liu-lakh ve]

Do I have to pay duty on these things?
Би эдгээр юманд татвар төлөх ёстой юу?
[bi ed-gEHr yu-mand tat-var tö-lökh yos-toi yUH]

How much do I have to pay in duty?
Хичнээн татвар төлөх вэ?
[khich-nEHn tat-var tö-lökh ve]

Getting around

A taxi service is available in Ulaanbaatar. For your convenience, you can catch a cab on the street. You can order a taxi twenty-four hours a day from the City Taxi Company (tel: 343433).

How can I get a taxi?
Такси яаж барих вэ?
[tak-si yAHj ba-rikh ve]

Where can I get a taxi?
Такси хаанаас барих вэ?
[tak-si khAH-nAHs ba-rikh ve]

Where is the taxi stand?
Таксины зогсоол хаана байна вэ?
[tak-si-ny zog-sOHl khAH-na bain ve]

Can you call a taxi for me?
Надад такси дуудаж өгнө үү?
[na-dad tak-si dUH-daj ög-nö üh]

Please give me the phone number of the taxi company.
Надад такси дуудах утасны номер өгнө үү?
[na-dad tak-si dUH-dakh u-tas-ny no-mer ög-nö üh]

The most popular form of public transportation in "UB" is the bus and the trolleybus. There is a bus stop every kilometer, but it is important to know your route.

Asking the way

I'm a foreigner.
Би гадааадын хүн.
[bi ga-dAH-dyn khün]

Excuse me, can you tell me where ... is?
... хаана байдгыг хэлж өгнө үү?
[... khAH-na baid-gyg khelj ög-nö üh]

... the post office
холбоо ...
[khol-bOH]

... the department store
их дэлгүүр ...
[ikh del-gÜHr]

... the food market
хүнсний зах ...
[khüns-nEE zakh]

... a business center
бизнесийн төв ...
[...biz-ne-sEEn töv]

... Datacom Computer Center
компьютерийн төв Датаком ...
[...kom-pyUH-te-rEEn töv datacom]

... Ulaanbaatar Hotel
Улаанбаатар зочид буудал ...
[u-lAHn-bAH-tar zo-chid bUH-dal]

How can I get from here to …?
   … руу яаж очихыг хэлж өгнө үү?
   [… ruh yAHj o-chi-khyg khelj ög-nö uh]

     … the Tuushin Restaurant
      Туушин ресторан …
      [tUH-shin res-to-rAHn]

     … the Emon Bar
      Эмон бар …
      [e-mOHn bar]

     … the stadium
      цэнгэлдэх хүрээлэн …
      [tsen-gel-dekh khü-rEH-len]

     … Mongolian State University
      Монгол улсын их сургууль …
      [mon-gol ul-syn ikh sur-gUHli]

     … Sukhbaatar Square
      Сүхбаатарын талбай …
      [sükh-bAH-ta-ryn tal-bai]

     … the train station
      вокзал …
      [vok-zAHl]

     … the airport
      онгоцны буудал …
      [on-gots-ny bUH-dal]

Write down the address for me, please.
   Хаягыг нь надад бичиж өгнө үү?
   [khaya-gyg ni na-dad bi-chij ög-nö uh]

I'm trying to locate this address.
   Би энэ хаягыг хайж байна.
   [bi e-ne khaya-gyg khaij bain]

I've lost my way.
Би төөрсөн байна.
[bi tÖHr-sön bain]

Is there a bus stop near here?
Автобусны буудал ойр байна уу?
[av-to-bus-ny bUH-dal oir bain uh]

Walking

Since everything is close by, the best way to see the sights in Ulaanbaatar is by walking. Walking helps put you in close contact with the people and gives you a wonderful opportunity to observe the Mongolian lifestyle and traditions. You should not be surprised to find many young people eager to practice their English! Here are some helpful expressions to use while sightseeing:

Where is ...?
... хаана байна вэ?
[khAH-na bain ve]

ask again when you see ...
... дэргэд очоод дахин асуу
[... der-ged o-chood da-khin a-suh]

across from
эсрэг талд
[es-reg tald]

around the corner
булан тойроод
[bu-lan toi-rOHd]

first left, then right
эхлээд зүүн, дараа нь баруун
[ekh-lEHd zühn, da-rAH ni ba-rUHn]

on the right
  баруун талд
  [ba-rUHn tald]

on the left
  зүүн талд
  [zühn tald]

make a U-turn
  буцаж эргэ
  [bu-tsaj er-ge]

make a right turn
  баруун тийш эргэ
  [ba-rUHn tEEsh er-ge]

make a left turn
  зүүн тийш эргэ
  [zühn tEEsh er-ge]

next to …
  … ний дэргэд
  [… nee der-ged]

straight ahead
  эгц урагшаа
  [egts u-rag-shAH]

ten meters from here
  эндээс арван метрт
  [en-dEHs ar-van metrt]

there
  тэнд
  [tend]

turn left at the first traffic light
  замын гэрлээр зүүн тийш эргэ
  [za-myn ger-lEHr zühn tEEsh er-ge]

Bus and trolleybus

Does this bus go to ...?
> Энэ автобус ... руу очих уу?
> [e-ne av-to-bUHs ... ruh o-chikh uh]

Which bus goes to ...?
> ... руу ямар автобус явдаг вэ ?
> [...ruh ya-mar av-to-bUHs yav-dag ve]

Where does the airport bus leave from?
> Онгоцны буудлын автобус хаанаас явдаг вэ?
> [on-gots-ny bUHd-lyn av-to-bUHs khAH-nAHs
>   yav-dag ve]

Where is the bus stop?
> Автобусны буудал хаана байдаг вэ?
> [av-to-buhs-ny bUH-dal khAH-na bai-dag ve]

Conductor!
> Кондуктор аа!
> [kon-dUHk-tor ah]

Two tickets, please.
> Хоёр билет авъя.
> [kho-yor bi-let av'ya]

Could you remind me when it is my stop?
> Миний буудал болохоор сануулна уу?
> [mi-nEE bUH-dal bo-lo-khOHr sa-nUHl-na uh]

How many stops to the...?
> ... руу хэдэн буудал вэ?
> [... ruh khe-den bUH-dal ve]

Train

One of the principal ways to travel in Mongolia is by train.
The capital of Mongolia is connected via the TransMongol
Railway to China and Russia, and the rail network

includes the local stations of Selenge, Darkhan, Airag, Sain-Shand, Zamyn Ühd and Erdenet. There are no trains further west than Erdenet. Trains from Moscow to Beijing run once a week in each direction and take about five days for the whole trip. Local trains run between Ulaanbaatar and Beijing.

Does the train go to …?
   … руу галт тэрэг явдаг уу?
   [… ruh galt te-reg yav-dag uh]

Where is the ticket office?
   Билет хаанаас авах вэ?
   [bi-let khah-nAHs a-vakh ve]

I'd like to get two tickets to Erdenet.
   Эрдэнэт руу хоёр билет авъя.
   [er-de-net ruh kho-yor bi-let av'ya]

How much does a compartment to Darkhan cost?
   Дархан руу купе ямар үнэтэй вэ?
   [dar-khan ruh ku-pEH ya-mar ü-ne-tei ve]

How many hours does it take to travel to Sain-Shand?
   Сайн Шанд руу хэдэн цаг явах вэ?
   [sain shand ruh khe-den tsag ya-vakh ve]

Excuse me, where is seat #4?
   4 дүгээр суудал хаана байна?
   [dö-röv dü-gEHr sUH-dal khah-na bain]

Can I get a clean sheet?
   Би цагаан хэрэглэл авъя
   [bi tsa-gAHn khe-reg-lel av'ya]

Could you give me some hot water?
   Халуун ус өгнө үү?
   [kha-lUHn us ög-nö üh]

When can I use the lavatory?
Жорлон хэзээ онгойх вэ?
[jor-lon khe-zEH on-goikh ve]

USEFUL VOCABULARY

airplane, plane
онгоц
[on-gots]

bag
цүнх
[tsünkh]

baggage check room
тээш хадгалах өрөө
[tehsh khad-ga-lakh ö-rÖH]

baggage claim
ачаа олгох
[a-chAH ol-gokh]

baggage ticket
ачааны талон
[a-chAH-ny ta-lon]

boarding pass
суух талон
[suhKH ta-lOHn]

bus
автобус
[av-to-bus]

bus stop
автобусны буудал
[av-to-bus-ny bUH-dal]

camera
зургийн аппарат
[zur-gEEn ap-pa-rat]

cargo
онгоцны ачаа тээш
[on-gots-ny a-chAH tehsh]

cart
түрдэг тэрэг
[tür-deg te-reg]

carton
цаасан хайрцаг
[tsAH-san khair-tsag]

citizen
иргэн
[ir-gen]

compartment
купе
[ku-pe]

conductor
кондуктор
[kon-dUHk-tor]

customs
гааль
[gAHli]

customs declaration
гаалийн мэдүүлэг
[gAH-lEEn me-dÜH-leg]

customs control
гаалийн шалгалт
[gAH-lEEn shal-galt]

customs inspection
гаалийн үзлэг
[gAH-lEEn üz-leg]

declaration
мэдүүлэг
[me-dÜH-leg]

declare
мэдүүлэх
[me-dÜH-lekh]

departure
хөөрөх
[khÖH-rökh]

departure gate
хөөрөх гарц
[khÖH-rökh garts]

embassy
элчин сайдын яам
[el-chin sai-dyn yAHm]

fill out a declaration
мэдүүлэг бөглөх
[me-dÜH-leg bög-lökh]

flight
нислэг
[nis-leg]

gate
хаалга
[khAHl-ga]

handbag
гар цүнх
[gar tsünkh]

information desk
лавлах товчоо
[lav-lakh tov-chOH]

luggage, baggage
ачаа, тээш
[a-chAH, tehsh]

narcotics, drugs *(illicit)*
мансууруулах бодис
[man-sUH-rUH-lakh bo-dis]

painting
зураг
[zu-rag]

passport
паспорт
[pahs-port]

passport control
паспортын шалгалт
[pahs-por-tyn shal-galt]

payment
төлбөр
[töl-bör]

perfume
үнэртэй ус
[ü-ner-tei us]

seat
суудал
[sUH-dal]

aisle seat
захын суудал
[za-khyn sUH-dal]

seat in the middle
дунд суудал
[dund sUH-dal]

window seat
цонхон талын суудал
[tson-khon ta-lyn sUH-dal]

seat in the nonsmoking area
тамхи татаж болох суудал
[tam-khi ta-taj bo-lokh sUH-dal]

seat in the smoking area
тамхи татаж болохгүй суудал
[tam-khi ta-taj bo-lokh-güi sUH-dal]

suitcase
чемодан
[che-mo-dahn]

taxi
такси
[tak-si]

ticket
тасалбар
[ta-sal-bar]

ticket office
тасалбар түгээх
[ta-sal-bar tü-gEHkh]

tobacco products
тамхин бүтээгдэхүүн
[tam-xin bü-tEHg-de-khÜHn]

train
галт тэрэг
[galt te-reg]

train station
  вокзал
  [vok-zAHl]

visa
  виз
  [viz]

  entry visa
    орох виз
    [o-rokh viz]

  transit visa
    дамжин өнгөрөх виз
    [dam-jin ön-gö-rökh viz]

vehicle
  автомашин
  [av-to-ma-shin]

weapons
  зэвсэг
  [zev-seg]

Money

The Mongolian unit of currency is the $T\Theta\Gamma P\Theta\Gamma$ [tög-rög].

Although the exchange rate fluctuates, over recent years it has stabilized to the point where US$1 is equivalent to approximately 1,100 tögrög (subject to daily fluctuation). Mongolians formerly had coins as part of their currency, but they were done away with in 1990. Since then, only bills—in denominations of 1, 5, 10, 20, 100, 500, 1000, 5000 and 10,000 tögrög—have been used. The currency symbol is a double-barred T.

For mostly practical considerations, the only place where you will be able to exchange your local currency for tögrög is Mongolia; foreign banks do not stock the currency. In Ulaanbaatar, you have basically two choices: one legal, the other somewhat less so. Legal outlets where you can exchange your local currency into tögrögs are the large banks in Ulaanbaatar, e.g. the Golomt Bank, the Trade and Development Bank, etc. Here you will receive the official rate of exchange. The other option, more lucrative for the foreigner, is to go to one of Ulaanbaatar's black markets. Although technically this is not legal, the authorities usually turn a blind eye to such transactions.

When exchanging money in Mongolia, whether at a bank or a black market, it is best to have crisp, new larger-denomination, banknotes, especially the newer-style $50- and $100-dollar bills. Torn or soiled banknotes, or those with writing on them, will not fetch the best exchange rates. Traveler's checks are also accepted in Ulaanbaatar's major banks, but probably nowhere else in Mongolia. Major credit cards are accepted at the capital's larger hotels and at a number of Western-style restaurants.

ATMs do not exist in Mongolia.

Where is there a bank near here?
Энд ойрхон банк байна уу?
[end oir-khon bank bain uH]

I want to exchange some money.
Би мөнгө солимоор байна.
[bi mön-gö so-li-mOHr bain]

I want to cash some traveler's checks.
Би аялалын чекээ мөнгө болгох гэсэн юм.
[bi a-ya-la-lyn che-kEH mön-gö bol-gokh ge-sen yum]

What is the rate of exchange today?
Өнөөдрийн ханш ямар байна?
[ö-nÖHd-rEEn khansh ya-mar bain]

How many *tögrög* per dollar?
Нэг доллар хэдэн төгрөг вэ?
[neg dol-lar khe-den tög-rög ve]

USEFUL VOCABULARY

bank
банк
[bank]

credit card
кредит карт
[kre-dit kart]

cash *n.*
бэлэн мөнгө
[be-len mön-gö]

cash *v.*
бэлэн мөнгө болгох
[be-len mön-gö bol-gokh]

cashier
касс
[kass]

change *v.*
солих
[so-likh]

money exchange point
мөнгө солих цэг
[mön-gö so-likh tseg]

rate of exchange
солих ханш
[so-likh khansh]

At the Hotel

As soon as you arrive at the airport in Ulaanbaatar, you can ask for directions to one of the hotels downtown. Some of the more popular hotels frequented by tourists to Mongolia are the Tuushin, Ulaanbaatar, Bayangol, and Chinggis Khan. English is spoken in all of these hotels and the service approximates what one would expect to find in a European or American hotel. All of these hotels contain restaurants and a business center, and the latter offer the possibility of sending and receiving faxes and e-mail. You can expect to pay from $25 to $100 for a one-night stay at a hotel in Mongolia's capital city.

The standard electrical voltage in Mongolia is 220V, 50 cycles/second, and it is supplied via Russian-style electricity outlets. The connector pins are round, usually 4 mm in diameter, and so you will probably need an adapter.

Where can I get information about hotels?
Зочид буудлын тухай мэдээлэл хаанаас авч болох вэ?
[zo-chid bUHd-lyn tu-khai me-dEH-lel khAH-nahs avch bo-lokh ve]

Where is the Bayangol Hotel?
Баянгол зочид буудал хаана байдаг вэ?
[Bayan-gol zo-chid bUU-dal khAH-na bai-dag ve]

How can I get to the Chinggis Khan Hotel?
Чингис зочид буудал руу яаж очих вэ?
[Ching-gis zo-chid bUH-dal ruh yAHj o-chikh ve]

Do you have any vacancies?
Танайд сул өрөө байгаа юу?
[ta-naid sul ö-röh bai-gAH yUH]

A room has been reserved for me at your hotel.
Миний өрөө захиалагдсан байгаа.
[mi-nEE ö-rÖH za-khia-lagd-san bai-gAH]

At the Hotel

I want a single room.
    Надад нэг ортой өрөө хэрэгтэй байна.
    [na-dad neg or-toi ö-rÖH khe-reg-tei bain]

I want a double room.
    Надад хоёр ортой өрөө хэрэгтэй байна.
    [na-dad kho-yor or-toi ö-rÖH khe-reg-tei bain]

Is there … in the room?
    Өрөөнд … байгаа юу?
    [ö-rÖHnd … bai-gAH yUH]

    … a TV
        … телевизор
        [te-le-vi-zor]

    … a telephone
        … утас
        [u-tas]

    … a radio
        … радио
        [ra-dio]

    … a refrigerator
        … хөргөгч
        [khör-gögch]

    … an air conditioner
        … агааржуулагч
        [a-gAHr-jUH-lagch]

Which floor is the room on?
    Өрөө маань хэдэн давхарт байдаг вэ?
    [ö-rÖH mAHni khe-den dav-khart bai-dag ve]

What is the room number?
    Өрөөний номер хэд вэ?
    [ö-rÖH-nii no-mer khed ve]

May I see the room?
Өрөөгөө үзэж болох уу?
[ö-rÖH-gÖH ü-zej bo-lokh uh]

Do I pay in advance?
Урьдчилан төлж болох уу?
[urid-chi-lan tölj bo-lokh uh]

This room suits (doesn't suit) me.
Энэ өрөө надад таарна (таарахгүй).
[e-ne ö-rÖH na-dad tAHr-na (tAH-rakh-güi)]

Don't disturb.
Саад бүү бол.
[Sahd büh bol]

Clean the room.
Өрөөг цэвэрлэнэ үү.
[ö-rÖHg tse-ver-le-ne üh]

When is checkout time?
Гарах цаг хэзээ вэ?
[ga-rakh tsag khe-zEH ve]

I'm leaving tomorrow at eight A.M.
Би маргааш өглөө найман цагт явна.
[bi mar-gAHsh ög-lÖH nai-man tsagt yav-na]

I'd like to pay the bill now.
Одоо тооцоогоо хиймээр байна.
[o-dOH tOH-tsOH-gOH khEE-mEHr bain]

Will you please prepare the bill by ten o'clock?
Тооцоогоо 10 цагт хийхээр бэлэн болгоно уу?
[tOH-tsOH-gOH ar-van tsagt khEE-kEHr be-len bol-go-no uh]

Can you call a taxi for me?
Надад такси дуудаж өгнө үү?
[na-dad tak-si dUH-daj ög-nö üh]

Do you have a business center?
Танайд бизнес төв бий юу?
[ta-naid biz-nes töv bee yUH]

Can I use the Internet?
Би Интернет хэрэглэж болох уу?
[bi in-ter-nEHt khe-reg-lej bo-lokh uh]

Can I use this hotel's e-mail address?
Буудлын И-майл хаягийг хэрэглэж болох уу?
[bUHd-lyn e-mail khay-gEEg khe-reg-lej bo-lokh uh]

USEFUL VOCABULARY

advertisement
зарлал
[zar-lal]

ad in a newspaper
сонины зарлал
[so-ni-ny zar-lal]

bar
бар
[bahr]

bathroom
угаалгын өрөө
[u-gAHl-gyn ö-rÖH]

bed
ор
[or]

king (queen)-size bed
том ор
[tom or]

double bed
хоёр ор
[kho-yor or]

single bed
ганц ор
[gants or]

twin bed
хоёр хүний ор
[kho-yor khü-nEE or]

bedding
орны цагаан хэрэглэл
[or-ny tsa-gAHn khe-reg-lel]

bill
тооцоо
[tOH-tsOH]

blanket
хөнжил
[khön-jil]

to book a room, to make a reservation
өрөө захиалах
[ö-rÖH za-khia-lakh]

café
зуушны газар, кафе
[zUHsh-ny ga-zar, ka-feh]

chair
сандал
[san-dal]

chambermaid
үйлчлэгч
[üilch-legch]

At the Hotel

to check in at a hotel
буудалд буух
[bUH-dald buhkh]

checkout time
гарах цаг
[ga-rakh tsag]

desk clerk, receptionist
бүртгэгч
[bürt-gegch]

door
хаалга
[khAHl-ga]

front door
гол хаалга
[gol khAHl-ga]

elevator
цахилгаан шат
[tsa-khil-gAHn shat]

exit
гарц
[garts]

fire
гал
[gal]

fire extinguisher
гал унтраагч
[gal unt-rAHgch]

floor
давхар
[dav-khar]

> first floor (ground floor)
> нэгдүгээр давхар
> [neg-dü-gEHr dav-khar]

> second floor
> хоёрдугаар давхар
> [kho-yor-du-gAHr dav-khar]

form
маягт
[ma-yagt]

> to fill out a form
> маягт бөглөх
> [ma-yagt bög-lökh]

guest
зочин
[zo-chin]

hair dryer
үсний сэнс
[üs-nEE sens]

hanger (clothes)
өлгүүр
[öl-gÜH]

hotel
зочид буудал
[zo-chid bUH-dal]

iron
индүү
[in-dÜH]

key
ТҮЛХҮҮр
[tül-khÜHr]

laundry service
угаалгын үйлчилгээ
[u-gAHl-gyn üil-chil-gEH]

lobby
ҮҮДНИЙ өрөө
[ÜHd-nEE ö-rÖH]

location
байршил
[bair-shil]

luggage, baggage
ачаа
[a-chAH]

    baggage check room
    ачаа хадгаламж
    [a-chAH khad-ga-lamj]

pay
төлөх
[tö-lökh]

    pay in advance
    урьдчилан төлөх
    [urid-chi-lan tö-lökh]

    pay cash
    бэлнээр төлөх
    [bel-nEHr tö-lökh]

plug *(electric)*
штепсель
[shtEHp-seli]

refrigerator
  хөргөгч
  [khör-gögch]

room
  өрөө
  [ö-rÖH]

roommate
  өрөөний хүн
  [ö-rÖH-nEE khün]

sauna
  саун
  [sa-UHn]

security
  аюулгүй байдал
  [a-yUHl-güi bai-dal]

service
  үйлчилгээ
  [üil-chil-gEH]

  room service
    өрөөнд үйлчлэх
    [ö-rÖHnd üilch-lekh]

shower
  шүршүүр
  [shür-shÜHr]

surcharge
  нэмэлт төлбөр
  [ne-melt töl-bör]

tax
  татвар
  [tat-var]

At the Hotel

telephone
утас
[u-tas]

> to make a telephone call
> утасдах
> [u-tas-dakh]

> to call from a room
> өрөөсөө ярих
> [ö-rÖH-nÖH-sÖH ya-rikh]

> to dial direct
> шууд залгах
> [shuhd zal-gakh]

telephone number
утасны дугаар
[u-tas-ny du-gAHr]

telephone conversation
утасны яриа
[u-tas-ny ya-ria]

> local call
> хот доторхи яриа
> [khot do-tor-khi ya-ria]

> long distance call
> хот хоорондын яриа
> [khot khoo-ron-dyn ya-ria]

> international call
> улс хоорондын яриа
> [uls khOH-ron-dyn ya-ria]

tip
цайны мөнгө
[tsai-ny mön-gö]

toilet, bathroom
жорлон, бие засах газар
[jor-lon, bi-ye za-sakh ga-zar]

men's room
эрэгтэй жорлон
[e-reg-tei jor-lon]

lady's room
эмэгтэй жорлон
[e-meg-tei jor-lon]

towel
алчуур
[al-chUHr]

traffic noise
гудамжны чимээ
[gu-damj-nEE chi-mEH]

valuables
үнэт зүйлс
[ü-net züils]

waiter, waitress
зөөгч
[zöhgch]

wake up
сэрээх
[se-rEHkh]

get a wake-up call
утсаар сэрээх
[ut-sAHr se-rEHkh]

water
ус
[us]

hot water
халуун ус
[kha-lUHn us]

cold water
хүйтэн ус
[khüi-ten us]

Food and Drink

Mongolians have their own quite unique foods and manner of preparing them. To a considerable degree this is the result of historical traditions and customs, which are intertwined with the lifestyle and harsh existence of the Mongolian people.

Mongolia is characterized by a severe Eurasian climate where the principal nomadic activity is animal husbandry. Consequently, it is a country where meat is a dietary staple. The most popular meat is mutton, followed by beef, pork and, over recent years, chicken. But it is not only the meat in a Mongolian's diet which is so important; of equal importance is the fat of the meat *өөx* [öhkh]. The importance of fat in a Mongolian's diet was initially conditioned by the rigors of nomadic life and the need to have a concentrated form of high-calorie energy.

Local cooking is quite distinctive. One local specialty is *Boodog*—whole carcass of goat roasted from inside with entrails and bones taken out through the throat. The carcass is filled with burning hot stones and the neck is tied tightly. Thus, the animal is cooked from the inside rather than the outside. River fish are also widely available. In addition to meat, the Mongolian diet consists of a number of dairy products characteristic of a nomadic existence but encountered throughout Mongolia. These include: dried curds *ааруул* [AH-rUHl], the skimmed portion of boiled milk *өрөм* [ö-röm], and yogurt *тараг* [ta-rag].

It is impossible to pay a visit to a Mongolian without being offered something to eat and drink. Indeed, in Mongolia it is unthinkable not to offer a guest, whether invited or uninvited, some refreshments. Invariably, the first thing a guest will be offered is Mongolian tea. This takes the form of very milky tea served with … salt. For most Westerners, Mongolian tea is an acquired taste. It is actually easier to get used to than it might seem at first, and it is both a refreshing beverage as well as a conversation backdrop. A similarly refreshing beverage, although of an entirely different nature, is fermented mare's milk—*айраг* [airag], also known by its Russian name kumiss. This mild beverage has a slightly acid taste, is a great thirst quencher, and is served in large bowls. If one drinks too much *airag*, one may easily become drunk since the drink may contain up to 18% alcohol, the equivalent of wine.

Other typical Mongolian dishes include:

бууз [buhz] (steamed dumplings)
хуушуур [xUH-shUHr] (elongated fried dumplings)
хуйцаа [xui-tsAH] (mixed soup)
цуйван [tsui-van] (steamed noodles with meat)

Western life is gradually making inroads into Mongolia, and one area where this can be seen is restaurants, most particularly, in Mongolia's capital city, Ulaanbaatar. As the administrative, economic, political and cultural center of Mongolia, Ulaanbaatar now boasts a large selection of non-Mongolian restaurants. These include Turkish, Chinese, French, German, Italian, Russian and Indian cuisine. As a landlocked country, Mongolia cannot offer its visitors fresh seafood, except in cans or as an expensive import, although the country's rivers teem with fish, white fish, perch and pike, for example.

Simple questions for orientation

Is there a restaurant in the hotel?
    Буудалд ресторан бий юу?
    [bUH-dald res-to-rAHn bee yUH]

Is there a coffee shop here?
    Энд кафе бий юу?
    [end ka-fe bee yUH]

When is breakfast served?
>Өглөөний цайны цаг хэзээ вэ?
>[ög-lÖH-nEE tsai-ny tsag khe-zEH ve]

Do you have room service?
>Өрөөнд очиж үйлчлэх үү?
>[ö-rÖHnd o-chij üilch-lekh ÜH]

In the restaurant

Waiter!
>Үйлчлэгч ээ!
>[üilch-legch EH]

Can we sit here?
>Энд сууж болох уу?
>[end suhj bo-lokh UH]

Could I see the menu, please?
>Хоолны цэс авч болох уу?
>[khOHl-ny tses avch bo-lokh uh]

What do you have for… ?
>Танайд ямар … байна вэ?
>[ta-naid ya-mar … bain ve]

>… breakfast
>>… өглөөний цай
>>[ög-lÖH-nEE tsai]

>… lunch
>>… өдрийн хоол
>>[öd-rEEn khohl]

>… dinner
>>… оройн хоол
>>[o-roin khohl]

Is fish on the menu today?
Өнөөдөр загас байгаа юу?
[ö-nÖH-dör za-gas bai-gAH yUH]

What would you like?
Та юу захиалах вэ?
[ta yUH za-khia-lakh ve]

I'd like a cup of tea.
Би аяга цай авъя.
[bi a-ya-ga tsai av'ya]

Where are the restrooms?
Бие засах газар хаана вэ?
[biye za-sakh ga-zar khAH-na ve]

USEFUL VOCABULARY

bread
талх
[talkh]

chewing gum
бохь
[bokhi]

cup
аяга
[aya-ga]

flour
гурил
[gu-ril]

fork
сэрээ
[se-rEH]

spoon
халбага
[khal-ba-ga]

glass
стакан
[sta-kan]

jam
чанамал, варенье
[cha-na-mal, va-rEHnie]

ketchup
кетчуп
[ket-chup]

knife
хутга
[khut-ga]

mustard
гич
[gich]

mayonnaise
майонез
[mai-OH-nez]

napkin
салфетка
[sal-fet-ka]

oil
тос
[tos]

plate
таваг
[ta-vag]

pepper
чинжүү
[chin-jÜH]

salt
давс
[davs]

soy sauce
цуу
[tsuh]

sugar
caaxap
[sAH-khar]

vinegar
цагаан цуу
[tsa-gAHn tsuh]

yeast
дрожжи
[drOHj-ji]

Drinks

brandy
бранди
[bran-dy]

beer
пиво
[pEE-vo]

champagne
шампанск
[sham-pAHnsk]

coffee
  кофе
  [kOH-fye]

juice *(fruit)*
  ЖИМСНИЙ ШҮҮС
  [jims-nEE shühs]

milk
  СҮҮ
  [süh]

soda
  ундаа
  [un-dAH]

spring water
  рашаан
  [ra-shAHn]

tea
  цай
  [tsai]

tonic
  ХИЙЖҮҮЛСЭН УС
  [khEE-jÜHl-sen us]

vodka
  архи
  [ar-khi]

water
  УС
  [us]

whisky
  виски
  [vis-ki]

wine
ВИНО
[vi-no]

sweet (red) wine
улаан вино
[u-lAHn vi-no]

dry wine
хуурай вино
[khUH-rai vi-no]

Dairy products

butter
масло
[mas-lo]

cheese
бяслаг
[byas-lag]

eggs
өндөг
[ön-dög]

boiled
чанасан
[cha-na-san]

fried
шарсан
[shar-san]

omelet
омлет
[om-let]

honey
зөгийн бал
[zö-gEEn bal]

milk
сүү
[süh]

yogurt
тараг
[ta-rag]

Meat and poultry

bacon
гахайн утсан мах
[ga-khain ut-san makh]

beef
үхрийн мах
[ükh-rEEn makh]

chicken
тахианы мах
[ta-khia-ny makh]

fish
загас
[za-gas]

hotdogs
зайдас
[zai-das]

horse meat
адууны мах
[a-dUH-ny makh]

lamb
хонины мах
[kho-ni-ny makh]

liver
элэг
[e-leg]

pork
гахайн мах
[ga-khain makh]

poultry
шувууны мах
[shu-vUH-ny makh]

sausages
хиам
[khi-ahm]

tongue
хэл
[khel]

veal
тугалын мах
[tu-ga-lyn makh]

Seafood

caviar
түрс
[türs]

crab
наймаалж
[nai-mAHlj]

fish
загас
[za-gas]

herring
май агас
[mai za-gas]

lobster
хавч
[khavch]

salmon
яргай загас
[yar-gai za-gas]

sardines
сардина
[sar-di-na]

shrimp
сам хорхой
[sam khor-khoi]

smoked fish
утсан загас
[ut-san za-gas]

taimen
тул
[tul]

white fish
цагаан загас
[tsa-gAHn za-gas]

Food and Drink

Vegetables

bean
буурцаг
[bUHr-tsag]

cabbage
байцаа
[bai-tsAH]

carrots
лууван
[lUH-van]

corn
эрдэнэ шиш
[er-de-ne shish]

cucumber
огурцы
[o-gur-tsy]

garlic
сармис
[sar-mis]

ginger
цагаан гаа
[tsa-gAHn gah]

lettuce
салад
[sa-lad]

mushroom
мөөг
[möhg]

olive
ЧИДУН
[chi-dun]

onion
СОНГИНО
[son-gi-no]

parsley
ЯНШУЙ
[yan-shui]

pea
ВАНДУЙ
[van-dui]

pickle
ДАРСАН НОГОО
[dar-san no-gOH]

potatoe
ТӨМС
[töms]

scallion
НОГООН СОНГИНО
[no-gOHn son-gi-no]

tomato
ЛООЛЬ
[lOHli]

turnip
МАНЖИН
[man-jin]

Fruits

apple
   алим
   [a-lim]

apricot
   абрикос
   [ab-ri-kOHs]

avocado
   авокадо
   [av-ko-da]

banana
   банан
   [ba-nAHn]

cherry
   интоор
   [in-tOHr]

grape
   усан үзэм
   [u-san ü-zem]

kiwi fruit
   киви
   [kEE-vi]

lemon
   нимбэг
   [nim-beg]

melon
   гуа
   [gua]

orange
  апельсин
  [a-peli-sin]

peache
  тоор
  [tohr]

peanut
  самар
  [sa-mar]

pear
  лийр
  [leer]

pineapple
  хан боргоцой
  [khan bor-go-tsoi]

plum
  чавга
  [chav-ga]

prune
  хар чавга
  [khar chav-ga]

raisin
  үзэм
  [ü-zem]

raspberry
  бөөрөлзгөнө
  [bÖH-rölz-gö-nö]

strawberry
  гүзээлзгэнэ
  [gü-zEHlz-ge-ne]

tangerine
мандарин
[man-da-rin]

watermelon
шийгуа
[shEE-gu-AH]

Desserts

Traditionally, desserts have never been a major focus of a Mongolian's diet. Over recent times, however, one effect of the mass media and international travel has been the growing popularity of Western-style desserts. This is especially so in Ulaanbaatar's many foreign restaurants.

cake
торт, бялуу
[tohrt, bya-lUH]

candy
чихэр
[chi-kher]

chocolate
шоколад
[sho-ko-lAHd]

ice cream
мөхөөлдөс
[mökh-ÖHl-dös]

fruit salad
жимсний салад
[jims-nEE sa-lAHd]

In conclusion

Enjoy your meal!
Сайхан хооллоорой!
[sai-khan khOHl-lOH-roi]

It was tasty.
Амттай байлаа
[amt-tai bai-lAH]

Could I have a second helping?
Дахин нэгийг авч болох уу?
[da-khin ne-gEEg avch bo-lokh UH]

The bill, please.
Тооцоогоо хийе
[tOH-tsOH-gOH khEE-ye]

Communication

Postal service

The Central Post Office in Ulaanbaatar is located next to
Sukhbaatar Square. In the main hall you will find postal
services as well as the "Mongol Shuudan Bank."

Where is the ... post office?
    ... шуудан хаана байдаг вэ?
    [... shUH-dan khAH-na bai-dag ve]

      ... general
        ... төв
        [töv]

      ... nearest
        ... ойролцоох
        [oi-rol-tsOHkh]

      ... branch # 13
        ... арван гуравдугаар салбар
        [ar-van gu-rav-du-gAHr sal-bar]

Where is the mail box?
    Шуудангийн хайрцаг хаана байна вэ?
    [shUH-dan-gEEn khair-tsag khAH-na bain ve]

When is the post office open?
    Холбооны газар хэзээ онгойх вэ?
    [khol-bOH-ny ga-zar khe-zEH on-goikh ve]

Where is the ... window?
    ... цонх хаана байна вэ?
    [tsonkh khAH-na bain ve]

      ... packages
        ... илгээмжийн
        [il-gEHm-jEEn]

... postal
   ... шуудангийн
   [shUH-dan-gEEn]

... special purpose
   ... тусгай үйлчигээний
   [tus-gai üil-chil-gEH-nEE]

Please send this by... mail.
   Үүнийг ... аар явуулна уу?
   [ÜH-nEEg ... ahr ya-vUHl-na uh]

... surface
   ... газраар
   [gaz-rAhr]

... air
   ... агаараар
   [a-gAH-rAhr]

... registered
   ... баталгаатай
   [ba-tal-gAH-tai]

... insured
   ... даатгалтай
   [dAHt-gal-tai]

How much is the postage for a letter to...?
   ... руу ямар үнээр явах вэ?
   [ruh ya-mar ü-nEHr ya-vakh ve]

... America
   ... Америка
   [a-me-ri-ka]

... England
   ... Англи
   [ang-li]

... Australia
... Австрали
[avst-rAH-li]

... New Zealand
... Шинэ Зеланд
[shi-ne ze-land]

... Beijing
... Бээжин
[bEH-jin]

... Japan
... Япон
[ya-pOHn]

How do I mail a package?
Би энэ боодлыг яаж явуулах вэ?
[bi e-ne bOHd-lyg yaj ya-vUH-lakh ve]

Give me ...
Надад ... өгнө үү!
[na-dad ög-nö üh]

... 1000-tögrög stamps
... мянган төгрөгний марк
[myan-gan tög-rög-nEE mark]

... an envelope with a stamp
... марктай дугтуй
[mark-tai dug-tui]

... ten postcards
... арван ил захидал
[ar-van il za-khi-dal]

Do you have other postcards I can look at?
Өөр ил захидал үзэж болох уу?
[öhr il za-khi-dal ü-zej bo-lokh uh]

Can I see …
   …үзэж болох уу?
   [ü-zej bo-lokh uh]

   … water color-painted postcards
   усан будгийн зураг…
   [u-san bud-gEEn zu-rag]

   … some commemorative stamps
   маркний цуглуулга…
   [mark-nEE tsug-lUHl-ga]

How much does it cost?
   Энэ ямар үнэтэй вэ?
   [e-ne ya-mar ü-ne-tei ve]

I like it.
   Надад таалагдаж байна.
   [na-dad tAH-lag-daj bain]

I'll take it.
   Би үүнийг авъя.
   [bi üh-nEEg av-ya]

Telephone, Fax and Internet

Long-distance communication between Mongolia and other countries of the world is completely up-to-date. Fax and e-mail are available in the capital as well as in the other two leading cities, Darkhan and Erdenet.

The major hotels have business centers with the latest technology for the use of their guests. Here you will also find Internet access.

One of the first and most popular Internet service provider companies is DataCom which is located east of Sukhbaatar Square. Here an Internet café equipped with PCs is available for your convenience. Another Internet café exists for the use of the public, but the most popular public source of Internet access is the Communication Center in the same building as Datacom. Internet access is usually charged by the hour, faxes by the page. Even if you need to pay a small fee for printing, still you will be happy to have computer access for such a low cost. Now they are offering reliable and inexpensive Internet phone calls to the USA and other parts of the world. For further information, visit the main Mongolian Web site: www.mol.mn.

Mobile phone services are available in Mongolia. Two leading cellular phone companies, MobiCom and SkyTel, have their offices just behind the Central Post Office and west of Sukhbaatar Square. These companies provide cellular phone services (GSM standard) in Ulaanbaatar, as well as Darkhan, Erdenet and some *aimag* centers. If you take your GSM mobile phone to Ulaanbaatar, you will be able to get a service contract which includes the appropriate chip card.

Answering the phone

Hello?
Байна уу?
[bain uh]

Is Dorj there?
Дорж байна уу?
[Dorj bain uh]

Yes, one moment, please.
Байна. Одоохон.
[bain. o-dOH-khon]

Speaking.
Би байна.
[bi bain]

No, he is not here.
Тэр энд байхгүй байна.
[ter end baikh-güi bain]

I'd like to talk to Mr. Chuluun.
Чулуун гуайтай ярья.
[Chu-lUHn guai-tai yari-ya]

Could you connect me with Mrs. Suren?
Сүрэн гуайтай холбож өгнө үү?
[Sü-ren guai-tai khol-boj ög-nö üh]

Can I call you back?
Би тань руу дараа залгаж болох уу?
[bi tani ruh da-rAH zal-gaj bo-lokh uh]

Can I leave a message for Mr. Tsend?
Би Цэнд гуайд захиа үлдээж болох уу?
[bi tsend guaid za-khia ül-dEHj bo-lokh uh]

Tell him to call Bat at …
Түүнд Бат руу … номероор утасдаарай гэж хэлнэ үү?
[tühnd Bat ruh …no-me-rOHr u-tas-dAH-rai gej khel-ne üh]

Thank you. Goodbye.
Баярлалаа. Баяртай
[ba-yar-la-lAH. ba-yar-tai]

Shopping

The main shopping center in Ulaanbaatar is the four-story State Department Store, which is located two blocks west of Sukhbaatar Square. The first floor contains the food section. On the second and third floors are clothing, jewelry, stationery, etc. On the fourth floor you can find duty-free goods and souvenirs. Highly recommended purchases in Mongolia are cashmere garments and camel-wool blankets, which are considered of the highest quality on the world market. Some local Mongolian products are national costumes, boots, jewelry, carpets, books, records and CDs, all of which are available at the State Department Store.

There are many duty-free shops where convertible currencies are accepted. The duty-free shops offer an extensive range of name brand cigarettes, gifts, pens, and liquors. In all other shops, local currency *tögrög* must be used. US$1 equals approximately 1,100 tögrög. (see "Money" section)

I've got some shopping to do.
  Би юм худалдан авмаар байна.
  [bi yum khu-dal-dan av-mAHr bain]

Is the State Department Store near here?
  Энд Их Дэлгүүр ойрхон байна уу?
  [end ikh del-gÜHr oir-khon bain UH]

Is there a market near here?
  Энд зах ойрхон байна уу?
  [end zakh oij-khon bain uh?]

Could you tell me where there is a … ?
  Хаана … байгааг хэлж өгнө үү?
  [… khAH-na bai-gAHg khelj ög-nö ÜH]

  … bookstore
    … номын дэлгүүр
    [no-myn del-gÜHr]

... grocery store
   ... ХҮНСНИЙ ДЭЛГҮҮР
   [khüns-nEE del-gÜHr]

... florist shop
   ... ЦЭЦГИЙН ДЭЛГҮҮР
   [tsets-gEEn del-gÜHr]

... pharmacy
   ... ЭМИЙН САН
   [e-mEEn san]

... school supply store
   ... бичиг хэрэглэлийн дэлгүүр
   [bi-chig khe-reg-le-lEEn del-gÜHr]

... jewelry shop
   ... алт мөнгөн эдлэлийн дэлгүүр
   [alt mön-gön ed-le-lEEn del-gÜHr]

... laundromat
   ... угаалгын газар
   [u-gAHl-syn ga-zar]

... dry cleaner's
   ... ХИМИ ЦЭВЭРЛЭГЭЭ
   [khi-mi tse-ver-le-gEH]

... shoe repair shop
   ... гутал засвар
   [gu-tal zas-var]

... hairdresser's
   ... ҮСЧИН
   [üs-chin]

... market
   ... зах
   [zakh]

... open air market
  ... гадаа зах
  [ga-dAH zakh]

Can I help you?
  Танд тусалж болох уу?
  [tand tu-salj bo-lokh uh]

Yes, please.
  За тэг.
  [za teg]

No, thanks. I'm just looking.
  Үгүй, баярлалаа. Би зөвхөн үзэж байна.
  [ü-güi, bayar-la-lAH. bi zöv-khön ü-sej bain]

Can you help me?
  Надад туслана уу?
  [na-dad tus-la-na UH]

How much does it cost?
  Энэ ямар үнэтэй вэ?
  [e-ne ya-mar ü-ne-tei ve]

It is too expensive.
  Маш их үнэтэй байна.
  [mash ikh ü-ne-tei bain]

I like it.
  Надад таалагдаж байна.
  [na-dad tAH-lag-daj bain]

Please show me.
  Надад үзүүлнэ үү?
  [na-dad ü-zÜHl-ne üh]

Could you reduce the price a bit?
  Үнээ буулгах уу?
  [ü -nEH bUHl-gakh uh]

I'll take it.
Би үүнийг авья.
[bi ÜH-nEEg avi-ya]

Do I pay you or at the cash register?
Мөнгөө кассанд төлөх үү, энд үү?
[mön-gÖH kah-sand tö-lökh üh, end üh)

Pack it for me, please.
Надад боож өгнө үү.
[na-dad bohj ög-nö üh]

Can I return this?
Үүнийг буцааж болох уу?
[ÜH-nEEg bu-tsAHj bo-lokh uh]

Can you put it in plastic bags, please?
Гялгар уутанд хийнэ үү?
[gyal-gar UH-tand khEE-ne üh]

At the department store

Where is the ... department?
... тасаг хаана байна вэ?
[ta-sag khAH-na bain ve]

    ... bedding
      ... орны
      [or-ny]

    ... books
      ... номын
      [no-myn]

    ... candy and sweets
      ... чихрийн
      [chikh-rEEN]

... cosmetics
   ... гоо сайхны
   [goh sai-kha-ny]

... children's
   ...ХҮҮХДИЙН
   [khÜHkh-dEEn]

... dairy goods
   ... цагаан идээний
   [tsa-gAHn id-EH-nEE]

... electric appliances
   ... цахилгаан барааны
   [tsa-khil-gAHn ba-rAH-ny]

... furs
   ... ҮСЛЭГ ЭДЛЭЛИЙН
   [üs-leg ed-le-lEEn]

... jewelry
   ...алт мөнгөний
   [alt mön-gö-nEE]

... ladies' clothing
   ... эмэгтэй хувцас
   [e-meg-tei khuv-tsas]

... lingerie
   ... дотуур хувцасны
   [do-tUHr khuv-tsas-ny]

... men's wear
   ... эрэгтэй хувцас
   [e-reg-tei khuv-tsas]

... shoe
   ... гутлын
   [gut-lyn]

... souvenir
    ... бэлэг дурсгалын
    [be-leg durs-ga-lyn]

... stationery
    ... бичгийн
    [bich-gEEn]

... toy
    ... тоглоомын
    [tog-lOH-myn]

... watch and clock
    ... цагны
    [tsag-ny]

Clothing

Salesperson!
    Худалдагч аа!
    [khu-dal-dagch AH]

I'd like to see ...
    Би ... үзмээр байна.
    [bi ... üz-mEHr bain]

    ... suits
        ... костюм
        [kos-tyum]

    ... dresses
        ... платье
        [plahti-ye]

    ... blouses
        ... нимгэн цамц
        [nim-gen tsamts]

... T-shirts
   ... футболк
   [fut-bohlk]

... shirts
   ... цамц
   [tsamts]

... skirts
   ... юбка
   [yuhb-ka]

... hats
   ... малгай
   [mal-gai]

... watches
   ... цаг
   [tsag]

... sweaters
   ... ноосон цамц
   [nOH-son tsamts]

... shoes
   ... ботинки
   [bo-tin-ki]

... boots
   ... гутал
   [gu-tal]

... underwear
   ... дотуур хувцас
   [do-tUHr khuv-tsas]

... socks
   ... оймс
   [oims]

... gloves
    ... бээлий
    [bEH-lEE]

I need a ... dress.
    Би ...н хувцас авмаар байна.
    [bi ...n khuv-tsas av-mAHr bain]

    ... cotton
        ... даавуу
        [dAH-vUHn]

    ... silk
        ... торго
        [tor-go]

    ... knitted
        ... нэхсэн
        [nekh-sen]

    ... woolen
        ... ноосон
        [nOH-son]

Souvenirs

I'm looking for ...
    Би ... хайж байна.
    [bi ... khaij bain]

    ... books
        ... ном
        [nom]

    ... a map
        ... газрын зураг
        [gaz-ryn zu-rag]

    ... ceramics
        ... шаазан
        [shAH-zan]

... a post card
    ... ил захидал
    [il za-khi-dal]

... a mask
    ... баг
    [bag]

... a ceramic camel
    ... шаазан тэмээ
    [shAH-zan te-mEH]

... a wood carving
    ... модон сийлбэр
    [mo-don sEEl-ber]

... a model of a *ger*
    ... гэрийн модель
    [ge-rEEn mo-deli]

... a doll
    ... хүүхэлдэй
    [khÜH-khel-dei]

... paintings
    ... зураг
    [zu-rag]

... a *deel (Mongolian garment)*
    ... Монгол дээл
    [mon-gol dehl]

... a chess set
    ... шатар
    [sha-tar]

... *Morin huur (a musical instrument)*
    ... морин хуур
    [mo-rin khUHr]

Medical Care

When traveling in another country, it is always wise to be prepared for medical emergencies. In Ulaanbaatar you are fortunate in that emergency medical services are readily available; however, when you travel outside Mongolia's capital city you should not rely on the availability of emergency medical services but rather be prepared to administer your own medical treatment in the case of an emergency.

Upset stomach complaints and hepatitis A are common in Mongolia. Potential travelers to Mongolia are advised to have hepatitis and tetanus inoculations before they travel.

It is strongly advised that *all* water be boiled before using. Rather than risk the danger of infection, be safe and try to buy bottled water and milk when available. Although it may not be easy to do this, try to avoid any dairy products made from unboiled milk.

Ensure that meat is thoroughly cooked.

When shopping in food stores, buy only well-packaged imported or domestic products with a "use by" date which has not expired. Fortunately, such products are in abundant supply in Ulaanbaatar and other cities.

Emergency care is available at the Russian hospital in Ulaanbaatar, although you may need an interpreter.

Travelers in winter should be aware of the danger of hypothermia, as the temperature can drop to minus 40 degrees Celsius.

It is highly recommended for all travelers to take an emergency medical kit with them. This should include such essential items as prescription and non-prescription medicines, aspirin, painkillers, Band-Aids, antibiotic ointment, bandages, diarrhea medication, laxatives and contraceptives. Note that after going to the bathroom, water for washing one's hands is not always available. To be on the safe side, it is better to take with you a hand sanitizer (liquid), wipes and deodorant. It is advisable to have a backup flashlight and batteries. Finally, don't forget your sunglasses.

When you are ill

Where is the clinic?
Эмнэлэг хаана байна вэ?
[em-ne-leg khAH-na bain ve]

How do I get to the hospital?
Би эмнэлэгт яаж очих вэ?
[bi em-ne-legt yAHj o-chikh ve]

How do I call a doctor?
Эмч яаж дуудах вэ?
[emch yAHj dUH-dakh ve]

Please call 103 for me.
Надад түргэн дуудаж өгнө үү?
[na-dad tür-gen dUH-daj ög-nö üh]

I need to see …
Надад … хэрэгтэй байна?
[na-dad … khe-reg-tei bain]

… a doctor
… эмч
[emch]

… a dentist
… шүдний эмч
[shüd-nEE emch]

... an eye doctor
  ... НҮДНИЙ ЭМЧ
  [nüd-nEE emch]

... a gynecologist
  ... ЭМЭГТЭЙЧҮҮДИЙН ЭМЧ
  [e-meg-tei-chÜHd-EEn emch]

Is there a doctor who speaks English?
  Англиар ярьдаг эмч олдох уу?
  [ang-liar yari-dag emch ol-dokh uh]

It's an emergency.
  Энэ маш яаралтай.
  [e-ne mash yAH-ral-tai]

At the doctor's office

Doctor!
  Эмч ээ!
  [emch EH]

Nurse!
  Сувилагч аа!
  [su-vi-lagch AH]

I feel completely exhausted.
  Би маш их ядарсан байна.
  [bi mash ikh ya-dar-san bain]

I have ...
  Миний ... өвдөж байна.
  [mi-nEE ... öv-döj bain]

... a headache
  ТОЛГОЙ
  [tol-goi]

... a stomachache
ГЭДЭС
[ge-des]

... a backache
нуруу
[nu-rUH]

... an earache
чих
[chikh]

I have a temperature.
Би халуунтай байна.
[bi kha-lUHn-tai bain]

I have a fever.
Би чичирч байна.
[bi chi-chirch bain]

I have a cough.
Би ханиалгаж байна.
[bi kha-nial-gaj bain]

I have a cold.
Би ханиадтай байна.
[bi kha-niad-tai bain]

I have a pain in my chest.
Миний цээж хөндүүрлэж байна.
[mi-nEE tsEhj khön-dÜHr-lej bain]

I have diarrhea.
Би суулгаж байна.
[bi sUHl-gaj bain]

I have insomnia.
Би нойр муутай байгаа.
[bi noir mUH-tai bai-gAH]

I feel sick.
> Бие тааруу байгаа.
> [bi-ye tAH-rUH bai-gAH]

I feel dizzy.
> Толгой эргээд байна.
> [tol-goi er-gEHd bain]

My throat is sore.
> Миний хоолой хөндүүр байна.
> [mi-nEE khOH-loi khön-dÜHr bain]

I'm sneezing a lot.
> Би олон найтааж байна.
> [bi o-lon nai-tAHj bain]

I'm constipated.
> Миний өтгөн хатсан.
> [mi-nEE öt-gön khat-san]

I've lost my appetite.
> Би хоолонд дургүй байна.
> [bi khOH-lond dur-güi bain]

I'm bleeding.
> Би цус алдаж байна.
> [bi tsus al-daj bain]

I'm dehydrated.
> Би шингэн алдсан.
> [bi shin-gen ald-san]

I have hypothermia.
> Би дулаанаа алдсан.
> [bi du-lAH-nAH ald-san]

I'm vomiting.
> Би бөөлжсөн.
> [bi bÖHlj-sön]

Medical Care

I cut my hand.
Би гараа эсгэсэн.
[bi ga-rAH es-ge-sen]

I've dislocated my arm.
Миний гар мултарсан.
[mi-nEE gar mul-tar-san]

I've sprained my ankle.
Миний шагай мултарсан.
[mi-nEE sha-gai mul-tar-san]

I'm taking this medicine.
Би энэ эмийг ууж байгаа.
[bi e-ne e-mEEg uhj bai-gAH]

I'm allergic to antibiotics.
Би антибиотикийн харшилтай.
[bi an-ti-bio-ti-kEEn khar-shil-tai]

How long should I take this medicine?
Энэ эмийг хир удаан уух вэ?
[e-ne e-mEEg khir u-dAHn uhkh ve]

How much is the fee?
Би хэдийг төлөх вэ?
[bi khe-dEEg tö-lökh ve]

When should I come back?
Би дахин хэзээ ирэх вэ?
[bi da-khin khe-zEH I-rekh ve]

At the dentist

What are the dentist's hours?
Шүдний эмч хэзээ ажилладаг вэ?
[shüd-nEE emch khe-zEH ajil-la-dag ve]

I have a toothache.
Миний шүд өвдөж байна.
[mi-nEE shüd öv-döj bain]

I broke my tooth.
Би шүдээ хугалчихлаа.
[bi shü-dEH khu-gal-chikh-lAH]

It hurts when I bite something.
Юм хазахаар өвдөөд байна.
[yum kha-za-khAHr öv-dÖHd bain]

I have bleeding gums.
Миний буйлнаас цус гарч байна.
[mi-nEE buil-nAHs tsus garch bain]

I've lost my false teeth.
Би хиймэл шүдээ гээчихлээ.
[bi khEE-mel shü-dEH gEH-chikh-lEH]

The crown has broken.
Холбоос нь хугарсан.
[khol-bOHs ni xu-gar-san]

I don't want to have the tooth pulled. Can you save it?
Би шүдээ авахуулмааргүй байна.
Та үлдээнэ үү?
[bi shü-dEH ava-khUHl-mAHr-güi bain.
ta ül-dEH-ne üh]

The filling fell out.
Би шүдээ хугалчихлаа.
[bi shü-dEH hu-gal-chikh-lAH]

Could you recommend a painkiller?
Өвчин намдаагч хэлж өгнө үү?
[öv-chin nam-dAHgch khelj ög-nö üh]

Medical Care

At the pharmacy

Where is the nearest pharmacy?
> Ойр эмийн сан байна уу?
> [oir e-mEEn san bain uh]

Do you have this medicine?
> Танайд энэ эм байна уу?
> [ta-naid e-ne em bain uh]

Please fill the prescription.
> Энэ жороор эм олгоно уу?
> [e-ne jo-rOHr em ol-go-no uh]

When will the medicine be ready?
> Эм хэзээ бэлэн болох вэ?
> [em khe-zEH be-len bo-lokh ve]

How much does the medicine cost?
> Эм ямар үнэтэй вэ?
> [em ya-mar ü-ne-tei ve]

How many times a day should I take the medicine?
> Эмийг өдөрт хэдэн удаа уух вэ?
> [e-mEEg ö-dört khe-den u-dAH uhkh ve]

I have a headache. What do you recommend?
> Миний толгой өвдөж байна. Юу уух вэ?
> [mi-nEE tol-goi öv-döj bain, yUH uhkh ve]

What could you recommend for me?
> Та надад юу уухыг хэлж өгнө үү?
> [ta na-dad yUH UH-khyg khelj ög-nö üh]

Are there special instructions for taking this medicine?
> Энэ эмийг уух тусгай заавар байна уу?
> [e-ne e-mEEg uhkh tus-gai zAH-var bain uh]

USEFUL VOCABULARY

abortion
   үр хөндөх
   [ür khön-dökh]

abscess
   буглаа
   [bug-lAH]

AIDS
   ДОХ
   [dokh]

acupuncture
   зүү эмчилгээ
   [züh em-chil-gEH]

allergy
   харшил
   [khar-shil]

allergy to medicines
   эмийн харшил
   [e-mEEn khar-shil]

allergy to pollen
   тоосны харшил
   [tOHs-ny khar-shil]

ambulance
   түргэн тусламж
   [tür-gen tus-lamj]

anesthesia
   унтуулах
   [un-tUH-lax]

Medical Care

local anesthesia
хэсгийн мэдээ алдуулах
[khes-gEEN me-dEH al-dUH-lakh]

antibiotic
антибиотик
[an-ti-bio-tik]

appendix
мухар олгой
[mu-khar ol-goi]

arm
гар
[gar]

artery
артерийн судас
[ar-te-rEEn sudas]

asthma
астм
[ah-stm]

back
нуруу
[nu-rUH]

bandage
боолт
[bOHlt]

Band-Aid
шархны лент
[sharkh-ny lehnt]

bleeding
цус алдах
[tsus al-dakh]

blind
    хараагүй, сохор
    [xa-rAH-güi, so-khor]

blood
    цус
    [tsus]

blood pressure
    цусны даралт
    [tsus-ny da-ralt]

    high blood pressure
        цусны даралт ихэдсэн
        [tsus-ny da-ralt i-khed-sen]

    low blood pressure
        цусны даралт багадсан
        [tsus-ny da-ralt ba-gad-san]

blood transfusion
    цус юүлэх
    [tsus yÜH-lekh]

blood test
    цусны шинжилгээ
    [tsus-ny shin-jil-gEH]

blood type
    цусны бүлэг
    [tsus-ny bü-leg]

body
    бие
    [bi-ye]

bone
    яс
    [yas]

breast
ХӨХ
[khökh]

burn
ТҮЛЭГДЭХ
[tü-leg-dekh]

capsule
ампул
[am-pUHl]

cast
ШОХОЙ
[sho-khoi]

to put on a cast
ШОХОЙДОХ
[sho-khoi-dokh]

cavity
ШҮДНИЙ ХОРХОЙ
[shüd-nEE khor-khoi]

chest
ЦЭЭЖ
[tsehj]

chronic
архаг
[ar-khag]

cold
ханиад
[kha-niad]

compress
ЖИН
[jin]

concussion
тархи хөдлөх
[tar-khi khöd-lökh]

condom
бэлгэвч
[bel-gevch]

constipation
өтгөн хатах
[öt-gön kha-takh]

cotton
хөвөн
[khö-vön]

cough
ханиалга
[kha-nial-ga]

cramp
шөрмөс татах
[shör-mös ta-takh]

deaf
дүлий
[dü-lEE]

dentist
шүдний эмч
[shüd-nEE emch]

diabetes
чихрийн шижин
[chikh-rEEn shi-jin]

diagnosis
онош
[o-nosh]

diarrhea
ГҮЙЛГЭХ
[güil-gekh]

disease
ӨВЧИН
[öv-chin]

childhood disease
ХҮҮХДИЙН ӨВЧИН
[khÜHkh-dEEn öv-chin]

contagious disease
халдварт ӨВЧИН
[khald-vart öv-chin]

dislocation
ҮЕ мултрах
[üye mult-rakh]

dizziness
ТОЛГОЙ ЭРГЭХ
[tol-goi er-gekh]

doctor
ЭМЧ
[emch]

dose
ТУН
[tun]

dropper
дусаагуур
[du-sAH-gUHr]

drops
дусаалга
[du-sAHl-ga]

dumb
ХЭЛГҮЙ
[khel-güi]

ear
ЧИХ
[chikh]

elbow
ТОХОЙ
[to-khoi]

eye
НҮД
[nüd]

eye doctor
НҮДНИЙ ЭМЧ
[nüd-nEE emch]

eyesight
хараа
[kha-rAH]

nearsightedness
ойрын хараа муу
[oi-ryn kha-rAH muh]

farsightedness
холын хараа муу
[kho-lyn kha-rAH muh]

feces
ӨТГӨН
[öt-gön]

fever
халууралт
[kha-lUH-ralt]

finger
   хуруу
   [khu-rUH]

flu
   грипп
   [grip]

fracture
   яс хугаралт
   [yas khu-ga-ralt]

furuncle
   хатиг
   [kha-tig]

gargle
   хоолой зайлах
   [khOH-loi zai-lakh]

glasses
   нүдний шил
   [nüd-nEE shil]

gums
   буйл
   [buil]

gynecologist
   эмэгтэйчүүдийн эмч
   [e-meg-tei-chÜH-dEEn emch]

head
   толгой
   [tol-goi]

hearing aid
   сонсголын аппарат
   [sons-go-lyn ap-raht]

heart
ЗҮРХ
[zürkh]

heart attack
ЗҮРХ ЗОГСОХ
[zürkh zog-sokh]

hemorrhoids
цагаан мах гарсан
[tsa-gAhn makh gar-san]

hepatitis
гепатит
[ge-pa-tit]

herbs
эмийн ургамал
[e-mEEn ur-ga-mal]

hoarseness
хоолой сөөх
[khOH-loi söhkh]

hospital
эмнэлэг
[em-ne-leg]

maternity hospital
амаржих газар
[a-mar-jikh ga-zar]

infection
халдвар
[khald-var]

inoculation
урдчилан сэргийлэх
[urd-chi-lan ser-gEE-lekh]

insomnia
нойргүйтэл
[noir-güi-tel]

inflammation
үрэвсэл
[ü-rev-sel]

inflammation of the prostate
түрүү булчирхайн үрэвсэл
[tü-rÜH bul-chir-khain ü-rev-sel]

inflammation of the bladder
давсагны үрэвсэл
[dav-sag-nEE ü-rev-sel]

injury
гэмтэл
[gem-tel]

insurance
даатгал
[dAHt-gal]

intestine
нарийн гэдэс
[na-rEEn ge-des]

itch
загатнаа
[za-gat-nAH]

kidney
бөөр
[böhr]

knee
өв-дөг
[öv-dög]

laxative
ӨТГӨН ХӨӨХ
[öt-gön khöhkh]

leg
ХӨЛ
[khöl]

liver
ЭЛЭГ
[e-leg]

loss of consciousness
ухаан алдах
[u-khAHn al-dakh]

lungs
уушиг
[UH-shig]

marmot plague
тарваган тахал
[tar-va-gan ta-khal]

medical history
ӨВЧНИЙ ТҮҮХ
[övch-nEE tühkh]

medicine
ЭМ
[em]

mixture
усан эм
[u-san em]

mouth
ам
[am]

muscle
булчин
[bul-chin]

nausea
бөөлжис цутгах
[bÖHl-jis tsut-gakh]

neck
хүзүү
[khü-zÜH]

needle
тариур
[ta-riur]

neurologist
мэдрэлийн эмч
[med-re-lEEn emch]

nurse
сувилагч
[su-vi-lagch]

optician
нүдний шилчин
[nüd-nEE shil-chin]

pain
өвдөх
[öv-dökh]

painkiller
өвчин намдаагч
[öv-chin nam-dAHgch]

patient
өвчтөн
[övch-tön]

period *(menstruation)*
   сарын тэмдэг
   [sa-ryn tem-deg]

pharmacist
   эмийн санч
   [e-mEEn sanch]

pill
   хуурай эм
   [khUH-rai em]

pharmacy
   эмийн сан
   [e-mEEn san]

pneumonia
   xatgaa
   [khat-gAH]

poisoning
   хордлого
   [khord-lo-go]

   food poisoning
      хоолны хордлого
      [khOHl-ny khord-lo-go]

pregnant
   жирэмслэлт
   [ji-rems-lelt]

prescription
   эмийн жор
   [e-mEEn jor]

prostate gland
   түрүү булчирхай
   [tü-rÜH bul-chir-kai]

pulse
судас
[su-das]

rabies
галзуурал
[gal-zUH-ral]

rheumatism
үе мөчний өвчин
[üye möch-nEE öv-chin]

salve, ointment
тосон түрхлэг
[to-son türkh-leg]

sedative
тайвшруулах
[taivsh-rUH-lakh]

shot (inoculation)
тариа
[ta-ria]

shoulder
мөр
[mör]

skin
арьс
[aris]

sleeping pills
нойрны эм
[noir-ny em]

smallpox
цагаан цэцэг
[tsa-gAHn tse-tseg]

sneeze
найтаалга
[nai-tAHl-ga]

sore
хөндүүр
[khön-dÜHr]

spleen
дэлүү
[de-lÜH]

splinter
өргөс
[ör-gös]

stomach
гэдэс, хомоод
[ge-des, kho-dOHd]

upset stomach
гэдэс өвдөх
[ge-des öv-dökh]

stroke
цус харвалт
[tsus khar-valt]

sunstroke
наранд цохиулах
[na-rand tso-khiu-lakh]

suppository
лаа
[lah]

surgeon
мэс засалч
[mes za-salch]

Medical Care

surgery
  хагалгаа
  [kha-gal-gAH]

swelling
  хаван
  [kha-van]

tablet, pill
  хуурай эм
  [khUH-rai em]

tears
  нулимс
  [nu-lims]

temperature
  халуун
  [kha-lUHn]

  to have one's temperature taken
    халуун хэмжих
    [kha-lUHn khem-jikh]

throat
  хоолой
  [khOH-loi]

thermometer
  халууны шил
  [kha-lUH-ny shil]

tooth
  шүд
  [shüd]

  upper tooth
    дээд шүд
    [dehd shüd]

lower tooth
ДООД ШУД
[dohd shüd]

front tooth
ҮҮДЭН ШУД
[ÜH-den shüd]

molar
араа
[a-rAH]

false teeth
ХИЙМЭЛ ШУД
[khEE-mel shüd]

toothache
ШУДНИЙ ӨВЧИН
[shüd-nEE öv-chin]

to pull out teeth
ШУД авах
[shüd a-vakh]

filling
пломбо
[plOHm-bo]

treatment
ЭМЧИЛГЭЭ
[em-chil-gEH]

ulcer
ходоодны шарх
[kho-dOHd-ny sharkh]

urine
ШЭЭС
[shehs]

uterus
умрээ
[üt-rEH]

vaseline
вазалин
[va-zah-lin]

vein
венийн судас
[ve-nEEn sudas]

vitamin
витамин
[vi-ta-mEEn]

vomiting
бөөлжих
[bÖHl-jikh]

womb
сав
[sav]

wound
шарх
[sharkh]

X ray
рентген
[rent-gEHn]

When someone sneezes, it is customary to say "Бурхан өршөө" [bur-khan ör-shÖH] (literally, God bless you).

Entertainment

Mongolia's capital city Ulaanbaatar offers performances at the State Opera and Ballet Theater, State Drama Theater, Puppet Theater and the Folk Song and Dance Ensemble. Even if you are not Mongolian and might not feel up to seeing a play, you most likely would enjoy a night at these theaters when a classical musical program is being performed, or if there are performances including unique folk songs with musical instruments. Circus entertainment also is very interesting.

Do you know of any good shows?
Сайхан үзвэр байна уу?
[sai-khan üz-ver bain uh]

What performance can you recommend?
Та ямар үзвэр санал болгох вэ?
[ta ya-mar üz-ver sa-nal bol-gokh veh]

Where can I get a ticket?
Тасалбар хаанаас авах вэ?
[ta-sal-bar khAH-nAHs a-vakh veh]

I'd like to see ...
Би ... үзмээр байна
[bi ... üz-mEHr bain]

　　... the opera
　　　... дуурь
　　　[duhri]

　　... classical music
　　　... сонгодог хөгжим
　　　[son-go-dog khög-jim]

　　... national folk songs
　　　... үндэсний дуу
　　　　[ün-des-nEE duh]

... the circus
   ... цирк
      [tsirk]

... the ballet
   ... балет
      [ba-lEHt]

... a play
   ... жүжиг
      [jü-jig]

If you go to a Mongolian national folk song concert, you will need to know some basic vocabulary.

throat song
   хөөмий
   [khÖH-mEE]

long song
   уртын дуу
   [ur-tyn duh]

folk dance
   ардын бүжиг
   [ar-dyn bü-jig]

contortion
   уран нугаралт
   [u-ran nu-ga-ralt]

Sightseeing in Ulaanbaatar

1. Museum of Fine Arts
2. Gandan Buddhist monastery
3. Temple of Megjid Janraisag
4. National Historical Museum

5. Bogd Khan Winter Palace Museum and *ger*

6. Natural History Museum

7. Sukhbaatar Square

8. Museum and exhibition of unique books in the State Central Library

9. Zaisan Monument (Zaisan Hill)

Tourist companies

There are several tourist companies operating remarkable sightseeing and adventure tours in Mongolia, and they proudly and graciously host travelers from all over the world.

They can offer you a range of classic tours featuring horse, yak, reindeer and camel treks, jeep adventures to the Gobi desert or to other natural beauty spots, or fishing, hiking and bicycling. The height of the tourist season is summer—June, July, August and September when the average temperature is 59° F.

Where can I find a tourist office?
Би жуулчны байгууллага хаанаас олох вэ?
[bi jUHlch-ny bai-gUHl-la-ga khAH-nAHs o-lokh veh]

I'd like to go sightseeing.
Би хот үзмээр байна.
[bi khot üz-mEHr bain]

What sights should we definitely see?
Ямар газрууд заавал үзэх ёстой вэ?
[ya-mar gaz-rUHd zAH-val ü-zekh yos-toi veh]

Can we get there by public transportation?
Тийшээ нийтийн унаагаар очиж болох уу?
[tEE-shEH nEE-tEEn u-nAH-gAHr o-chij bo-lokh uh]

Is there an excursion to ... we can take?
Бид хамт явбал ... руу экскурс байна уу?
[bid khamt yav-bal ... ruu eks-kurs bain uh]

  ... the Museum of Fine Arts
    ... уран зургийн музей
    [u-ran zur-gEEn mu-zei]

  ... the "Gandan" monastery
    ... Гандан хийд
    [gan-dan khEEd]

  ... Bogd Khan's Palace
    ... Богд хааны ордон
    [bogd khAH-ny or-don]

  ... the black market
    ... хар зах
    [khar zakh]

Can I hire a guide?
Тайлбарлагч авч болох уу?
[tail-bar-lagch avch bo-lokh uh]

Can I have an itinerary, please?
Аялалын хувиар авч болох уу?
[a-ya-la-lyn khu-viar avch bo-lokh uh]

Is there an art gallery in the city?
Энэ хотод зургийн үзэсгэлэн байна уу?
[e-ne kho-tod zur-gEEn ü-zes-ge-len bain uh]

I'd like to visit a ...
Би ... үзмээр байна.
[bi üz-mEHr bain]

  ... modern art exhibition
    ... орчин үеийн зургийн үзэсгэлэн
    [or-chin üye-EEn zur-gEE üzes-ge-len]

... museum
   ... музей
   [mu-zei]

... movie
   ... кино
   [ki-no]

... opera
   ... дуурь
   [duuri]

... ballet
   ... балет
   [ba-leht]

... comedy
   ... хошин урлаг
   [kho-shin ur-lag]

... gallery
   ... галерей
   [ga-le-rei]

... entertainment
   ... үзвэр
   [üz-ver]

Where is the Natural History Museum?
   Байгалын түүхийн музей хаана байдаг вэ?
   [bai-ga-lyn tÜH-khEEn mu-zei khAH-na bai-dag ve]

I'd like to see dinosaur skeletons.
   Би динозаврийн яс үзмээр байна.
   [bi di-no-zav-rEEn yas üz-mEHr bain]

Can we take a picture?
   Энд зураг авч болох уу?
   [end zu-rag avch bo-lokh uh]

In the Countryside

Outside Ulaanbaatar and other administrative centers you can see the traditional lifestyle of herdsmen, many of whom are nomadic, and live in a *ger* (yurt). Travel agencies offer trips to some interesting places like Terelj, the tourist camp closest to Ulaanbaatar; Kharkhorin, former capital of the Great Mongolian Empire; Lake Khobsgol, Amarbayasgalant Monastery, the Gobi Desert and Khan Khenti, the native land of Chinggis Khan.

Here is some vocabulary which will help you find a common language with Mongolian herdsmen:

Show me the countryside, please?
 Надад хөдөөг үзүүлнэ үү?
 [na-dad khö-dÖHg üz-ÜHl-ne üh]

I'd like to ride a horse.
 Би морь уная.
 [bi mori u-na-ya]

Could you help me?
 Та надад туслана уу?
 [ta na-dad tus-la-na uh]

Could I have some *airag*?
 Надад айраг өгнө үү?
 [na-dad ai-rag ög-nö üh]

I'm hot. Let's go to the river.
 Би халууцаж байна. Гол руу явъя.
 [bi kha-lUh-tsaj bain. gol ruh yav-ya]

Let's take a picnic dinner to the countryside.
 Хөдөө гарч оройн хоолоо идье.
 [khö-dÖH garch o-roin khOH-lOH id'ye]

I enjoyed myself very much. Thank you for your
hospitality.
Надад таатай байлаа. Зочилсонд тань их
баярлалаа.
[na-dad tAH-tai bai-lAH. zo-chil-sond tani ikh
ba-yar-la-lAH]

Do you have deerstone in this country?
Энэ нутагт буган хөшөө бий юу?
[ene nu-tagt bu-gan khö-shÖH bee yUH]

If you travel to Khövsgöl Aimag you will have a chance
to meet the Darkhat people (population: 4,500), a
Mongol-speaking ethnic group which lives by herding
reindeer; however, they also engage in other traditional
Mongolian activities. They are originally Lamaist Buddhist or shamanist. It is interesting to visit here during the
ovoo, water spirit and fire rituals.

Could you tell me about your traditions?
Та надад ёс заншлаасаа ярьж өгнө үү?
[ta na-dad yos zansh-lAH-sAH yarij ög-nö üh]

Can I ride a reindeer?
Цаа буга унаж болох уу?
[tsah bu-ga u-naj bo-lokh uh]

Tell me about this ritual.
Энэ ёслолын тухай хэлнэ үү?
[e-ne yos-lo-lyn tu-khai khel-ne üh]

It's very interesting.
Надад их сонин байна.
[na-dad ikh so-nin bain]

USEFUL HINT

Electricity is available in the cities of Mongolia as well as
in *aimag* centers and larger villages; in the countryside,
however, solar-driven batteries and flashlights are
extremely useful.

Festivals and Holidays

Naadam

If you travel to Mongolia during the summer you probably will see the Big Mongolian Holiday—*Naadam*,
which means "to play" or "to have an enjoyable time".
The Naadam Festival is one of the most exciting and col-
orful celebrations in Mongolia. It has been celebrated on
July 11-12 every year since the 1921 Mongolian Revolution. The events—the Three Manly Games—include
wrestling, horse racing and archery.

The wrestlers in Mongolia are very highly regarded and
they can have titles like "the Falcon" [na-chin], "the Elephant" [zahn], "the Lion" [ars-lan] and "the Giant" [a-var-
ga], depending on how many rounds they have won.

In order to win a title, wrestlers must fight their way
through 512 (!) competitors in a knockout competition
spread out over nine rounds.

The "Giant" title belongs to a person who wins at least
twice during the nine rounds.

The most exciting part of the Three Manly Games is
horse racing which involves only boys and girls aged
three to seven. Distances vary according to the age of the
horse. The shortest distance is 15 kilometers, the longest
is over 30 kilometers. Horse races are held in about six
categories with horses being two, three, four and six
years old.

Archery, the last of the Three Manly Games, enjoys
somewhat less popularity. It is certainly the quietest of all
three sports. On the other hand, age counts for a lot since
it is not strength but experience and good eyesight that
make winners.

The following questions and answers are the traditional greeting at Naadam:

Are you enjoying Naadam?
Сайхан наадаж байна уу?
[sai-khan nAH-daj bain uh]

Yes, I'm having a great time.
Сайхан наадаж байна.
[sai-khan nAH-daj baina]

Enjoy the Naadam celebrations.
Сайхан наадаарай!
[sai-khan nAH-dAH-rai]

Additional useful words and expressions during Naadam include the following:

wrestler
бөх
[bökh]

trainer
засуул
[za-sUHl]

winner
давсан бөх
[dav-san bökh]

loser
унасан бөх
[u-na-san bökh]

eagle dance
дэвэх
[de-vekh]

shoulder vest
зодог
[zodog]

snug shorts
шуудаг
[shUH-dag]

boots
гутал
[gu-tal]

holds
мэх
[mekh]

title
цол
[tsol]

Falcon
начин
[na-chin]

Elephant
заан
[zahn]

Lion
арслан
[ars-lan]

Giant
аварга
[a-var-ga]

archer
харваач
[khar-vAHch]

target
бай
[bai]

to hit the target
байг онох
[baig o-nokh]

accurate shooter (marksman)
мэргэн харваач
[mer-gen khar-vAHch]

child rider
хурдан морины хүүхэд
[khur-dan mo-ri-ny khÜH-khed]

saddle
эмээл
[e-mehl]

foal
унага
[u-na-ga]

one-year-old foal
даага
[dAH-ga]

two-year-old horse
шүдлэн
[shüd-len]

three-year-old horse
хязаалан
[khya-zAH-lan]

four-year-old horse
соёолон
[so-yo-lon]

five-year-old horse
хуучин соёолон
[khUH-chin so-yo-lon]

horse older than five years
ИХ НАСНЫ МОРЬ
[ikh nas-ny mori]

stallion
азарга
[a-zar-ga]

mare
ГҮҮ
[güh]

Tsagaan Sar (Mongolian Lunar New Year)

Tsagaan Sar literally means "white moon" because Mongolians compare purity and happiness with the color white. For more than 2,000 years, Mongols have been celebrating Tsagaan Sar to mark the end of the cold winter and the beginning of the spring thaw. This three-day holiday usually occurs in February when we say farewell to the animal sign of the outgoing year and welcome in the animal sign of the new year. The twelve animal signs are as follows: Rat, Bull, Tiger, Rabbit, Dragon, Snake, Horse, Ram, Monkey, Cock, Dog and Pig. On Lunar New Year's Eve, *Bituun*, the last day of the year, families gather around the table for a richly served dinner which includes two large dishes: one is a dish with molded pastry fried in oil; the other contains the carcass of a sheep. On the morning of the first day of the New Year close family members gather together to begin the New Year greeting process. This starts with an expression of deep respect paid to the oldest family member, who is offered *khadag* (Buddhist silk) or money. People celebrate the first day of spring and the New Year by partaking of enormous amounts of food and drink. Exchanging gifts is also part of the New Year's celebrations. Note the following special greetings on Tsagaan Sar:

How do you do?
Амар байна уу?
[a-mar bain uh]

Is your livestock fattened up nicely? Are you having a
good New Year's celebration?
Тарган орж, сайхан шинэлэв үү?
[tar-gan orj sai-khan shi-ne-lev üh]

Yes, they're all fattened up nicely, and we're having a
good celebration.
Тарган орж, сайхан шинэллээ.
[tar-gan orj sai-khan shi-nel-lEH]

Was your livestock in good shape?
Даага далантай, бяруу булчинтай юу?
[dAh-ga da-lan-tai bya-rUH bul-chin-tai yUH]

USEFUL PHRASES FOR TSAGAAN SAR:

to celebrate Tsagaan Sar
шинэлэх
[shi-ne-lekh]

to greet at the New Year
золгох
[zol-gokh]

steamed dumpling
бууз
[buhz]

molded pastry fried in oil
ул боов
[ul bohv]

dish of dairy foods
цагаалга
[tsa-gAhl-ga]

carcass of a sheep
ууц
[uhts]

Mongolian Holidays
(БАЯРЫН ӨДРҮҮД)

January 1 (Western) New Year's Day
Шинэ жил
[shi-ne jil]

February (day depends on lunar calendar)
Lunar New Year
Цагаан сар
[tsa-gAHn sar]

1st Sunday of February
National Teacher's Day
Багш нарын баяр
[bagsh na-ryn ba-yar]

March 8
Women's Day
Эмэгтэйчүүдийн баяр
[e-meg-tei-chÜH-dEEn ba-yar]

March 18
Soldier's Day
Цэргийн баяр
[tser-gEEn ba-yar]

April 1
April Fool's Day
Инээдмийн өдөр
[i-nEHd-mEEn ö-dör]

June 1
Children's Day
Хүүхдийн баяр
[khÜHkh-dEEn ba-yar]

July 11, 12, 13
Naadam (national holiday)
Үндэсний баяр Наадам
[ün-des-nEE ba-yar NAH-dam]

September 1
First day of school
Хичээлийн анхны өдөр
[khi-chEH-lEEn ankh-ny ö-dör]

November 26
Independence Day
Тусгаар тогтнолын өдөр
[tus-gAHr togt-no-lyn ö-dör]

Media

Publications

Among the better-known English-language newspapers published in Mongolia are "Mongol Messenger" and "Business Times," which are available at city newsstands.

Do you have the latest issue of "Mongol Messenger"?
"Монгол элч" сонины сүүлийн дугаар байна уу?
[mon-gol elch so-ni-ny sÜH-lEEn du-gAHr bain uh]

How much does it cost?
Ямар үнэтэй вэ?
[ya-mar ü-ne-tei ve]

I'll take it.
Би үүнийг авъя.
[bi ÜH-nEEg av-ya]

Do you have any other English-language newspapers or magazines?
Англи хэл дээр өөр хэвлэл байна уу?
[AHng-li khel deer öhr khev-lel bain uh]

What is available in other languages?
Өөр хэл дээр хэвлэл байна уу?
[öhr khel dehr khev-lel bain uh]

Radio

The most popular radio stations are FM 102.5 and 107.5. In their programs you can listen to Mongolian pop, rock music and other types of music from around the world.

The radio station "Voice of Mongolia" broadcasts eight hours a day in Mongolian, English, Chinese, Russian and Japanese.

Also, international shortwave broadcasts by "Radio Ulaan-baatar" can be heard daily in English and Mongolian from Australia, South Asia, Europe and North America.

Television

Cable TV, which features dozens of programs from around the world, is available in Ulaanbaatar and other cities in Mongolia.

Numbers, Days and Months

The cardinal numbers are as follows:

zero	ТЭГ [teg]
one	НЭГ [neg]
two	хоёр [kho-yor]
three	гурав [gu-rav]
four	дөрөв [dö-röv]
five	тав [tav]
six	зургаа [zur-gAH]
seven	долоо [do-lOH]
eight	найм [naim]
nine	ес [yös]
ten	арав [a-rav]
eleven	арван нэг [ar-van neg]
twenty	хорь [khori]
twenty-two	хорин хоёр [kho-rin kho-yor]

thirty	гуч	[guch]
forty	дөч	[döch]
fifty	тавь	[tavi]
sixty	жар	[jar]
seventy	дал	[dal]
eighty	ная	[na-ya]
ninety	ер	[er]
one hundred	нэг зуу	[neg zuh]
one hundred one	нэг зуун нэг	[neg zuhn neg]
two hundred	хоёр зуу	[xo-yor zuh]
three hundred	гурван зуу	[gur-van zuh]
four hundred	дөрвөн зуу	[dör-vön zuh]
five hundred	таван зуу	[ta-van zuh]
six hundred	зургаан зуу	[zur-gAHn zuh]
seven hundred	долоон зуу	[do-lOHn zuh]
eight hundred	найман зуу	[nai-man zuh]

Numbers, Days and Months

nine hundred	есөн зуу [yö-sön zuh]
one thousand	нэг мянга [neg myan-ga]

One hundred thousand seven hundred thirty-five
    Нэг зуун мянга долоон зуун гучин тав
    [neg zuhn mayn-ga dol-OHn zuhn guch-in tav]

Days of the Week

Monday	Даваа [da-vAH]
Tuesday	Мягмар [myag-mar]
Wednesday	Лхагва [l-khav-ga]
Thursday	Пүрэв [pü-rev]
Friday	Баасан [bAH-san]
Saturday	бямба [byam-ba]
Sunday	Ням [nyam]

These are the official names of the days of the week. In everyday Mongolian, however, people use the ordinal numbers 1 to 5 to designate Monday through Friday. The ordinal number is then followed by the word өдөр [ö-dör]. Thus,

Monday	нэгдэх өдөр [neg-dekh ö-dör]

Tuesday	хоёрдохь өдөр [kho-yor-dokhi ö-dör]
Wednesday	гурав дахь өдөр [gu-rav dakhi ö-dör]
Thursday	дөрөв дэхь өдөр [dö-röv dekhi ö-dör]
Friday	тав дахь өдөр [tav dakhi ö-dör]

For **Saturday** Mongolians say хагас сайн өдөр [xagas sain ö-dör] which means "half good day," and for **Sunday** they say бүтэн сайн өдөр [bü-ten sain ö-dör] "whole good day." In Mongolia the week begins on Monday and finishes on Sunday.

Months of the Year

Months in Mongolian are designated descriptively by ordinal number "month". For example, January (first month).

January	нэгдүгээр сар [neg-dü-gEHr sar]
February	хоёрдугаар сар [kho-yor-du-gAHr sar]
March	гуравдугаар сар [gu-rav-du-gAHr sar]
April	дөрөвдүгээр сар [dö-röv-dü-gEHr sar]
May	тавдугаар сар [tav-du-gAHr sar]

June	зургадугаар сар
	[zur-ga-du-gAHr sar]
July	долдугаар сар
	[dol-du-gAHr sar]
August	наймдугаар сар
	[naim-du-gAHr sar]
September	есдүгээр сар
	[yös-dü-gEHr sar]
October	аравдугаар сар
	[a-rav-du-gAHr sar]
November	арван нэгдүгээр сар
	[ar-van neg-du-gEHr sar]
December	арван хоёрдугаар сар
	[ar-van kho-yor-du-gAHr sar]

Monday, January 20, 2003
2003 оны 1 сарын 20, Даваа

Хоёр мянга гурван оны нэгдүгээр сарын
   хорин Даваа гариг.
[xo-yor myan-ga gur-van o-ny neg-dü-gEHr saryn
   kho-rin, dav-AH garig]

(In the above example, the Mongolian order of elements
is year, month, date, day.)

Measures and Sizes

The Metric System

MEASURES:

Mongolia uses the metric system of weights and measurements. You will need to know a few equivalents. Here are some of the basic ones:

Table 1

1 kilo(gram) = 2.2 pounds	1 pound = .45 kilo(gram)
1 liter = .55 pints	1 pint = 1.81 liters
1 liter = .26 gallons	1 gallon = 3.785 liters
0° C = 32° F	0 ° F = -17.7° C
37° C = 98.7° F	32° F = 0° C
1 centimeter = .39 inches	1 inch = 2.54 centimeters
1 kilometer = .62 miles	1 mile = 1.6 kilometer

SIZES:

S small (10-12)	жижиг [ji-jig]
M medium (14-16)	дунд [dund]
L large (18)	том [tom]
XL extra large (20-22)	маш том [mash tom]

In Table 2 you can see the differences between American and Mongolian clothing and shoe sizes.

Measures and Sizes

Table 2

Women's clothing		Men's clothing		Men's shirts	
Mongolian size	American size	Mongolian size	American size	Mongolian size	American size
36	8	50	40	36	14
38	10	52	42	37	14.5
40	12	54	44	38	15
42	14	56	46	39	15.5
44	16	58	48	40	16
46	18			41	16.5
48	20			42	17
				43	17.5

Table 3

Women's shoes		Men's shoes	
Mongolian size	American size	Mongolian size	American size
35	5	39	6.5
36	5.5	40	7.5
37	6	41	8.5
38	7	42	9
39	7.5-8	43	10
40	8.5	44	10.5
41	9	45	11

Colors
(ӨНГӨ)

black	хар [khar]
blue	хөх [khökh]
bronze	хүрэл [khü-rel]
brown	хүрэн [khü-ren]
gold	алтан [al-tan]
gray	буурал [bUH-ral]
green	ногоон [no-gOHn]
light blue	цэнхэр [tsen-kher]
magenta	хурц ягаан [khurts ya-gAHn]
orange	улбар шар [ul-bar shar]
pink	ягаан [ya-gAHn]
red	улаан [u-lAHn]
silver	мөнгөлөг [mön-gö-lög]
violet	чирнелин ягаан [chir-ne-lin ya-gAHn]

white	цагаан
	[tsa-gAHn]
yellow	шар
	[shar]

Visiting a Nomad's *Ger*

1. When you approach a *ger* make some noise: clear your throat or say "Nokhoi khorio" ("Hold back the dog") even if you don't see a dog. This is how the host knows that someone is coming. When the hosts hear you, they can prepare themselves to come out and meet you.

2. If you see livestock supplies (poles, whips for driving animals, etc.) on the ground around the *ger*, don't walk over them. Just walk around them.

3. The door of the *ger* is very low, so lower your head as you enter. Otherwise, you may hit your forehead.

4. Don't step on the threshold of the *ger*.

5. Don't enter the *ger* with your sleeves rolled up.

6. If you have any tools, instruments or weapons, leave them outside of the *ger*.

7. Once you are inside the *ger* don't wait for an invitation. Move around to the left and take a seat.

8. However much of a hurry you may be in, never leave the *ger* without first sampling whatever food your hosts have prepared. If you don't, your action will be considered bad luck.

9. If the host hands you a snuff box, take it in your open palm. Then take off the cap, have a sniff, lightly replace the cap and then hand it back.

10. When the hostess serves tea or *airag* in a bowl, she will hand it to you with both hands or with the bowl in the right hand while supporting her right elbow with her left hand. The guest must accept the host's

offering with both hands or with the right hand supported by the left hand.

11. As far as gifts are concerned, they are given and received as described above.

12. When you receive gifts, make sure your sleeves are rolled down, and don't be in a hurry to open the gifts. They should never be opened in the presence of the person who gave them to you.

Glossary of Cultural Terms

ааруул [AH-rUHl] *n.* hard dried milk curd

аварга [a-var-ga] *n.* Titan, the title for a wrestler who wins all encounters over two consecutive Naadams

авга [av-ga] *n.* relatives on the father's side: **авга ах** [av-ga akh] father's brother; **авга эгч** [av-ga egch] father's sister

азарга адуу [a-zar-ga a-dUH] *n.* herd of horses with one head stallion

аймаг [ai-mag] *n.* name of largest administrative division of Mongolia. Each of the 21 *aimags* is divided into *sums*

айраг [ai-rag] *n.* drink made from fermented mare's milk

алд [ald] *n.* unit of length measured between tips of outstretched arms

араг [a-rag] *n.* basket for collecting *argal*

аргал [ar-gal] *n.* dried cow or horse dung used for fuel

арслан [ars-lan] *n.* Lion, the title for a wrestler who wins all encounters during one Naadam

баг [bag] *n.* smallest administrative division in a *sum*; each *sum* has 4-5 *bag*.

Буриад [bu-ri-ad] *n.* second largest Mongolian minority group *(after Khalkh)*

бууз [buhz] *n.* steamed dumplings filled with chopped meat and onions

боодог [bOH-dog] *n.* whole carcass of goat or marmot roasted with hot stones from the inside with entrails and bones first removed through the throat

боов [bohv] *n.* molded pastry fried in oil

боорцог [bOHr-tsog] *n.* pastry deep fried in oil *(eaten throughout the day by the typical Mongolian family)*

борц [borts] *n.* strips of dried meat *(prepared in winter)* (similar to beef jerky)

бүлүүр [bü-lÜHr] *n.* paddle for making *airag*

бүрхээр [bür-khEHr] *n.* brewing cask for making home-made vodka *(shimiin arkhi)*

гөлөм [gö-löm] *n.* leather saddlecloth

гэр [ger] *n.* Mongolian-style circular dwelling with lattice sides covered by hides or felt, ideally suited for nomadic lifestyle. May be erected and disassembled in a matter of hours.

дархад [dar-khad] *n.* Mongolian minorities in Renchin-lkhumbe and Ulaan-Uul *sum* in Khövsgöl *aimag*

дэвэх [de-vekh] *n.* eagle dance, preceding and following wrestling competitions

дээл [dehl] *n.* traditional Mongolian outer garment worn by men, women and children. A lighter version is worn during the summer, a heavier one during the colder months.

> **дан дээл** [dan dehl] single *deel* made entirely from silk or linen. It is worn like a dress under the heavy deel on festive occasions and for ornamentation.

> **тэрлэг дээл** [ter-leg dehl] summer *deel* made from two materials and worn in summer by men, women and children

> **хөвөнтэй дээл** [khö-vön-tei dehl] cotton *deel* made from two layers of material and with cotton between. It is convenient to wear on colder days and between seasons.

> **үстэй дээл** [üs-tei dehl] skin *deel* made from the insides of sheep and lamb skins. Often worn during cold weather. Furs of wild animals are sometimes used.

> **дээлийн нударга** [deh-lEEn nu-dar-ga] extended part of sleeve cuff of a man's *deel* in the shape of a horse's hoof

заан [zahn] *n.* Elephant, the title for a wrestler who wins seven rounds

зах [zakh] *n.* flea market. There are two kinds of flea markets in Mongolia: хүнсний зах [khüns-nEE zakh] a food market; барааны зах [ba-rAH-ny zakh] an open-air market

золгох [zol-gokh] *v.* When greeting each other at New Year's, Mongolians employ a tradition dating back thousands of years—*zolgokh*. The traditional Mongolian New Year's greeting is highly structured and takes the following form. Two people walk toward each other. When they come face to face and only a short distance separates them, the younger of the two people takes into the palms of his hands the elbows of the older person. Then the older person kisses the younger person on the cheek. During this process, the older person says "Амар байна уу?" [a-mar bain uh] and the younger replies "Амар байна аа" [a-mar bain ah]. When the two people first approach each other, it is customary for the younger person to present the older person with *хадаг*, which may contain some (paper) money. The older person takes the *хадаг* and the money and folds and keeps them.

Some additional comments: Should two people be the same age, one of them cups the other's lowered elbow in the palm of his hand, while the other person cups the raised elbow of his coeval in the palm of his hand.

Husband and wife never greet each other in the *zolgokh* tradition.

зодог [zodog] *n.* Mongol wrestler's shoulder vest. It has an open chest, because the tale is told that a former tournament winner was a woman. Only men are permitted to wrestle.

зул [zul] *n.* Buddhist home-made candle for offering in *tsögts*. The wick is made from cotton; butter or vegetable oil are used for burning.

жирэм [ji-rem] *n.* the two left-side girths of a saddle

Казах [ka-zakh] *n.* Turkic-speaking Moslems concentrated in Bayan Ulgii *aimag*. They comprise 6% of the population.

Монголын нууц товчоо [mon-go-lyn nuuts tov-chOH] *n.* "The Secret History of the Mongols" is the greatest Mongolian historical book which has been preserved from ancient times. It was written in the thirteenth century by an unknown author. In this book, all of Chinggis Khan's (A.D. 1162–1227) ancestors, descendants, life and times, as well as the politics, economy and society of the time are described. This work is not only a significant source of historical pride for Mongols, but also provides the world with the best and most authoritative account of the Mongol empire in the thirteenth century.

морин хуур [mo-rin khuhr] *n.* musical instrument: horse-headed fiddle

мянгад [myan-gat] *n.* one of the Mongolian minorities

наадам [nAH-dam] *n.* known as the *eriin gurvan naadam*, after the "three manly sports" of wrestling, archery and horse racing. The festival is held all over the country, normally between July 11 and 12, the anniversary of the Mongolian Revolution in 1921.

нагац [na-gats] *n.* relatives on the mother's side. E.g., нагац ах [na-gats akh] mother's brother; нагац эгч [na-gats egch] mother's sister

начин [na-chin] *n.* Falcon, the title for a wrestler who wins five matches in succession

овоо [o-vOH] *n.* pile of sacred rocks, sometimes with a stick in the center, which have flags attached.

олом [o-lom] *n.* right-hand saddle girth

өрөм [ö-röm] *n.* skimmed portion of boiled milk

саадаг [sAH-dag] *n.* quiver with arrows

соёмбо [so-yom-bo] *n.* state emblem of Mongolia

сум [sum] *n.* small administrative subdivision of an *aimag*. Each *aimag* has approximately 10 to 15 *sum*. *Sum* is divided into *bags*.

сүүтэй цай [sÜH-tei tsai] *n.* tea with salt, milk and butter

таван хошуу мал [ta-van xo-shUH mal] *n.* livestock, specifically five kinds of domesticated animals: horse, cow, camel, sheep and goat

тавгийн идээ [tav-gEEn i-dEH] *n.* plate with food offered to guests

тооно [tOH-no] *n.* smoke hole of a *ger* named "window of heaven" or roof ring (hub)

торгууд [tor-gUHd] *n.* one of the Mongolian tribes

тохом [to-khom] *n.* camel saddle blanket

уурга [UHr-ga] *n.* Mongolian lasso. A long stick with a loop on the end

ууц [uhts] *n.* sheep carcass

халх [khalkh] *n.* dominant nationality in central Mongolia

халаг [kha-dag] *n.* scarf-like piece of fine loosely woven silken material or welcome cloth. A *khadag* expresses the highest form of respect and is frequently used when offering a toast to a respected guest or friend. The *khadag* is widely used by the Tibetans and the Mongols, as well as other Altaic people. *Khadag* come in several different colors, but mainly blue, white, gold and orange. They are used in temples where they are often draped over idols, and in the home. *Khadags* are also frequently found draped over sacred trees and *ovoo*.

When offering a *khadag* to someone, it is held in both hands together with a silver bowl containing milk or money in the right hand.

халуун хошуутай мал [kha-lUHn xo-shUH-tai mal] *n.* warm-muzzled beasts: sheep, horse, cow

хана [khana] *n.* lattice walls of a *ger*

хоймор [khoi-mor] *n.* back of a *ger*. This is the proper place for the head of the household, elders and one's most treasured possessions. On the back wall is the family altar, containing Buddhist images and family photos.

хүйтэн хошуутай мал [khüi-ten xo-shUH-tai mal] *n.* cold-muzzled beasts: camel, goat

хоргол [khor-gol] *n.* dried camel, sheep or goat dung

хөхүүр [khö-hÜHr] *n.* large animal skin bag for fermented *airag*

хуйцаа [xui-tsAH] *n.* mixed soup served with fatty sheep tail

хурал [khu-ral] *n.* meeting: Их Хурал [ikh khu-ral] Parliament

хуушуур [xUH-shUHr] *n.* elongated fried dumplings

цагаалга [tsa-gAhl-ga] *n.* dish of dairy foods served during *Tsagaan Sar*

цагаан сар [tsagaan sar] *n.* White Month. This is the start of the lunar New Year in January or February. After months of enduring a bitter winter, Mongolians celebrate over three days by consuming a great deal of food and drink.

цам [tsam] *n.* dances performed to exorcise evil spirits, influenced by Lamaism and Shamanism

цөгц [stögts] *n.* bowl for holding a *zul* religious offering

цуйван [tsui-van] *n.* steamed noodles with meat and vegetables

шагай [sha-gai] *n.* sheep's anklebones that Mongolians use in a number of games

шагай харвах [sha-gai khar-vakh] *n.* a game involving casting of anklebones

шуудаг [shUH-dag] *n.* snug shorts worn by Mongol wrestlers

шээзгий [shEHz-gEE] *n.* dung basket

шимийн архи [shi-mEEn ar-khi] *n.* home-brewed vodka from *airag* or yogurt, whose alcohol content is as high as 12%.

шинэлэх [shi-nel-ekh] *v.* to celebrate *Tsagaan Sar*

ээзгий [EHz-gEE] *n.* hard chunks of dried cheese

Further Reading
on Mongolia . . .

IMPERIAL MONGOLIAN COOKING

Recipes from the Kingdoms of Genghis Khan

Marc Cramer

This book is one of the first to explore the ancient cuisine of the Mongolian empire, opening a window onto a fascinating culture and a diverse culinary tradition virtually unknown to the West. These 120 easy-to-follow recipes encompass a range of dishes—from "Bean and Meatball Soup," to "Turkish Swordfish Kebabs." The recipes are taken from the four *khanates* (kingdoms) of the empire.

211 pages • 6 x 8¾ • illustrations •
0-7818-0827-8 • $24.95 • W • (20)

Hippocrene Language Guides to China and Russia

CANTONESE BASIC COURSE

416 pages • 5½ x 8½ •
0-7818-0289-X • $19.95pb • W • (117)

BEGINNER'S CHINESE

173 pages • 5½ x 8½ •
0-7818-0566-X • $14.95pb • W • (690)

CHINESE HANDY DICTIONARY

2,000 entries • 120 pages • 5 x 7¾ •
0-87052-050-4 • $8.95pb • USA • (347)

CHINESE-ENGLISH FREQUENCY DICTIONARY

500 entries • 167 pages • 6 x 9 •
0-7818-0820-0 • $14.95pb • W • (277)

ENGLISH-CHINESE PINYIN DICTIONARY

10,000 entries • 500 pages • 4 x 6 •
0-7818-0427-2 • $19.95pb • USA • (509)

HIPPOCRENE CHILDREN'S ILLUSTRATED CHINESE (MANDARIN) DICTIONARY
English-Chinese/Chinese-English

500 entries/illustrations • 94 pages • 8½ x 11 •
0-7818-0848-0 • $11.95pb • W • (662)

RUSSIAN-ENGLISH/ENGLISH-RUSSIAN STANDARD DICTIONARY
Revised Edition with Business Terms

32,000 pages • 418 pages • 5½ x 8½ •
0-7818-0280-6 • $18.95pb • W • (322)

RUSSIAN-ENGLISH COMPREHENSIVE DICTIONARY

40,000 entries • 844 pages • 6 x 9 • W
hardcover: 0-7818-0506-6 • $60.00 • (612)
paperback: 0-7818-0560-0 • $35.00 • (689)

ENGLISH-RUSSIAN COMPREHENSIVE DICTIONARY

50,000 entries • 804 pages • 6 x 9 •
0-7818-0442-6 • $35.00pb • W • (50)

RUSSIAN PHRASEBOOK AND DICTIONARY, REVISED

3,000 entries • 228 pages • 5½ x 8½ •
0-7818-0190-7 • $11.95pb • W • (597)
Cassettes: 0-7818-0192-3 • $12.95 • (432)

Hippocrene Children's Illustrated Russian Dictionary
English-Russian/Russian-English

500 entries/illustrations • 94 pages • 8½ x 11 •
0-7818-0892-8 • $11.95pb • W • (216)

Dictionary of 1,000 Russian Proverbs

181 pages • 5½ x 8½ •
0-7818-0564-3 • $11.95pb • W • (694)

Beginner's Russian

200 pages • 5½ x 8½ •
0-7818-0232-6 • $9.95pb • W • (61)

Mastering Russian

278 pages • 5½ x 8½ •
0-7818-0270-9 • $14.95pb • W • (11)
2 cassettes: 0-7818-0271-7 • $12.95 • (13)

All prices are subject to change without prior notice. To order **Hippocrene Books**, contact your local bookstore, call (718) 454-2366, visit www.hippocrenebooks.com, or write to: Hippocrene Books, 171 Madison Avenue, New York, NY 10016. Please enclose check or money order adding $5.00 shipping (UPS) for the first book and $.50 for each additional title.